Enhancing India-Central Asia Engagement: Prospects and Issues

Enhancing India-Central Asia Engagement: Prospects and Issues

Editor

Prof Nirmala Joshi

(Established 1870)

United Service Institution of India (USI)

Vij Books India Pvt Ltd

New Delhi (India)

Published by

Vij Books India Pvt Ltd
(Publishers, Distributors & Importers)
2/19, Ansari Road
Delhi – 110 002
Phones: 91-11-43596460, 91-11-47340674
Fax: 91-11-47340674
e-mail: vijbooks@rediffmail.com
we b: www.vijbooks.com

CONTENTS

APPROACH PAPER

ENHANCING INDIA-CENTRAL ASIA ENGAGEMENT: PROSPECTS AND ISSUES

1.   The Central Asian nations have been undergoing the process of nation building for the last two decades. Within this short period of time they have made considerable progress in many areas of human endeavour. As is the worldwide trend; economic, conventional security and non-traditional security issues have been the focus of much attention by the political leadership of these states. Every nation in the Central Asian region has unique characteristics and it pursues policies designed to benefit its people while attempting to enhance security and stability of the country and in the region. While Kazakhstan, Uzbekistan and Turkmenistan are rich in hydrocarbons, Tajikistan and Kyrgyzstan have abundant hydro power potential. Uzbekistan has the largest population base and Kazakhstan has the highest GDP in the region. Due to shared economic, political and security linkages of the past, they are mutually inter-dependent in many ways. Thus the Central Asian nations share a vision of regional cooperation.

2.   To take advantage of the rapidly globalizing world the Central Asian nations have been broadening their engagement with the outside world. Seeking multi-faceted engagement with outside powers enables them to widen their policy choices and usher in a certain degree of equilibrium in the region. On the other hand many major powers have promoted a number of competing multilateral security and economic structures possibly to secure their own geo-political interests. Nevertheless, Central Asian Republics view their membership of such structures as being advantageous to pursuing their interests in many ways.

3.   Despite a rich history of economic and cultural linkages with Central Asian Republics in the past the Indian engagement in

the current times leaves lot to be desired. However, India considers Central Asia as part of its extended/ strategic neighbourhood. Central Asian Republics and India have many mutual interests. Their relations are based on a shared commitment to open progressive societies, secularism, democracy, and improving the lot of the common people and the same has been reinforced by similarity of views in the fight against terrorism, drug trafficking and in many other areas of security.

4.   The unstable situation in Afghanistan is inextricably linked with India's and Central Asian Republic's security concerns, as Afghanistan is part of the larger Central Asian construct. In Afghanistan the three major challenges of governance, neutralizing the Taliban and economic development continue to be issues of grave concern for the people of Afghanistan and for countries that have a stake in the stability and security of that nation. The last decade has seen positive as well as not so positive developments in Afghanistan. How the dice will roll after 2014 is a subject of intense speculation in capitals around the globe.

5.   While security and stability in the region is of prime importance to the Central Asian Republics and India, the other important driving factor of the emerging relationship is the economic engagement. India seeks partnership within areas such as information technology, science and technology, knowledge industries etc. Conversely, India's increasing need for energy can be addressed by the energy-rich Central Asian countries. In the energy sector, there have been missed opportunities in the past, but India is striving to revitalize its interaction with concerned countries of Central Asia. Areas such as energy, non-conventional sources of energy and agro-based industries are promising spheres for cooperation. Joint ventures can be established which could benefit the entire region. However, lack of direct connectivity hampers interaction.

6.   There is a need to connect India with Central Asia through multi-modal corridors particularly in the transport and trade sectors. In a sense, it recreates the past history of the region when robust trading activity was a dominant feature. Afghanistan was the fulcrum on which such activities were carried out in various directions.

However, unstable situation in Afghanistan and obtuse policies of Pakistan prevent achievement of good connectivity between South and Central Asia.

7. Broadly the seminar on enhancing India- Central Asia engagement is built around the theme of security and stability, enhancing economic engagement including the energy sector and increasing connectivity to promote trade and commerce. These broad themes would contain many other sub-themes for widening the India-Central Asia engagement and the way ahead in Afghanistan.

PARTICIPANTS

Lieutenant General PK Singh, PVSM, AVSM (Retd)

Lieutenant General PK Singh was commissioned as a 2/Lt in the Indian Army in 1967. He retired as an Army Commander (C-in-C) in 2008. He is a graduate of Higher Command Course and the National Defence College. His academic qualifications include MSc; MPhil and Post-graduate Diploma in Business Management.

He took over as Director of the United Service Institution of India in January 2009. He is a member of the IISS, London and a Council Member of the Indian Council of World Affairs, New Delhi. He is an Adviser to the Fair Observer, USA.

His articles have been published in "The NIDS Journal", Tokyo; in "Global Security – The Growing Challenges", USA; and has written for the book, "The China-India Nuclear Crossroads" edited by Lora Saalman. He has written a chapter for the forthcoming "Oxford handbook on UN Peacekeeping Operations". He has edited the book "Comprehensive National Power – A Model for India" and the book "Civilian Capacity Building for Peace Operations".

He has participated in international conferences and seminars in USA, China, South Korea, Japan, Russia, Brazil, Norway, Sweden, Switzerland, South Africa, Ethiopia, Turkey, Germany, Austria, France, Bangladesh, Taiwan, Afghanistan, Kazakhstan, UAE, Australia etc.

Shri Sanjay Singh, Secretary (East), MEA

Mr. Sanjay Singh joined the Indian Foreign Service in 1976. He has served in Indian Missions in Mexico, Germany, Ghana and France and in the Ministry of External Affairs, New Delhi as Director in the Office of the External Affairs Minister and Joint Secretary and Head of Division dealing with Latin American Countries and later Establishment. From October 1997 to June 2001, he was

India's Consul General in Ho Chi Minh City and from July 2001 to August 2004, Deputy Chief of Mission in Paris. He served as Joint Secretary and Additional Secretary for Gulf and Haj from March 2005 to March 2009. He served as Ambassador of India to Iran from March 2009 to March 2011. He took over as Secretary (East) in the Ministry of External Affairs on 18th March 2011. Shri Sanjay Singh has a Masters in Physics from Delhi University.

Shri Ashok Sajjanhar, IFS (Retd)

Mr. Ashok Sajjanhar, who has Honours and Masters Degree in Physics from Delhi University, commenced his service career as a Staff Officer in Bank of India. Switching to a career in diplomacy, Mr. Sajjanhar has held various significant positions in Indian Embassies in Moscow, Teheran, Geneva, Dhaka, Bangkok, Washington, Brussels and Astana. Mr. Sajjanhar's professional interests include International Trade and during his assignment in Geneva from 1988 to 1992, he made significant contribution while representing India in the Uruguay Round of Multilateral Trade negotiations.

Mr. Sajjanhar has been an active participant in various International Seminars organized by UNCTAD and WTO. He has participated as Resource Person and Speaker at several Conferences on the Multilateral Trading System in Beijing, Kuala Lumpur, Bangkok, Papua New Guinea, Seoul, Geneva, etc. A keen proponent of Indian culture, he was the Director of Jawaharlal Nehru Cultural Centre in Moscow where he was instrumental in ushering in a new paradigm in cultural diplomacy.

Mr. Sajjanhar was the Deputy Chief of Mission as well as the Deputy Permanent Representative of India to UN-ESCAP during his assignment in Bangkok from 2000 to 2003. He was Deputy Chief of Mission in the Mission to European Union, Belgium and Luxemburg from 2005 to 2007 and Ambassador of India to Kazakhstan from 2007 to 2010.

Major General BK Sharma, AVSM, SM** (Retd)

Major General BK Sharma was commissioned in infantry in 1976 and commanded 6 SIKH LI. He holds double degree of MPhil and is pursuing his PhD in Geopolitics in Central Asia. He is a graduate of

Staff College, Higher Command and National Defence College. He attended a course in International Peacekeeping in Santiago (Chile) in the year 2000. He has tenanted prestigious command, instructional and staff appointments, notably, Senior Faculty Member at National Defence College, New Delhi, Command of a Mountain Division and Brigadier General Staff (both assignments on China Border) 'Principal Director Net Assessment at HQ Integrated Defence Staff, Defence Attaché in Embassy of India in Kazakhstan and Kyrgyzstan, and UN Military Observer in Central America.

He regularly contributes articles to prestigious journals. He lectures at prestigious think tanks in India, UN Research and Training Centre, New Delhi and at various universities in India and abroad. He regularly participates in international seminars.

He was awarded AVSM, SM and bar to SM by the President of India for courage and exceptional devotion to duty.

Presently, he is working as Distinguished Fellow at the United Service Institution of India, New Delhi. He specializes in Net Assessment, Scenario Building and Strategic Gaming. He conducts strategic games for the National Defence College and Higher Command Courses of the Army, Navy and Air Force.

Shri Yogendra Kumar, IFS (Retd)

Experience: Important Service Appointments

1987-1990   Consul General of India for the Central Asian region, Tashkent, USSR.

1990-1993   First Secretary/Counsellor, High Commission of India, Islamabad.

1993-1996   Director, Central Asia Division, Ministry of External Affairs, New Delhi.

1996-2000   Minister (Political Affairs), Embassy of India to the European Union, Belgium and Luxembourg, Brussels.

2000-2003   Ambassador of India in Tajikistan.

2003-2006   High Commissioner of India in Namibia.

2006 -2008   Senior Directing Staff [Foreign Service],
                 National Defence College, New Delhi.

2008-2009   Additional Secretary [Multi-lateral Economic
                 Relations], Ministry of External Affairs,
                 New Delhi.

2009-2012   Ambassador of India to the Philippines
                 with concurrent accreditation to Palau,
                 Federated States of Micronesia and the
                 Marshall Islands.

He speaks Russian language fluently and is also familiar with Tajik language. He retired from the Indian Foreign Service on 29 February, 2012.

Lieutenant General PC Katoch, PVSM, UYSM, AVSM, SC (Retd)

Lieutenant General PC Katoch, PVSM, UYSM, AVSM, SC, superannuated as DG Information Systems of Indian Army in 2009. A Special Forces officer, he fought in the 1971 India-Pakistan War, commanded an independent commando company in insurgency area, a Special Forces Battalion under the IPKF in Sri Lanka, a Brigade on Siachen Glacier, a Division in Ladakh and a Strike Corps in South Western Theatre. He has served as Defence Attache in Japan with accreditation to Republic of Korea and has held numerous operational staff appointments from Brigade HQ level to HQ IDS. An MSc in Defence Studies, he is an alumni of the Defence Services Staff College, Senior and Higher Command Courses and National Defence College. Post retirement, he has authored over 230 articles on military, security, topical and technical issues and as a Defence Analyst is a visiting scholar to foreign Think Tanks. He is member of the USI Council, an active participant in seminars at national and international levels and has co-authored a book on India's Special Forces.

Lieutenant General Vinay Shankar, PVSM, AVSM, VSM (Retd)

Lieutenant General Vinay Shankar retired from the Indian Army in December, 2000 after 40 years of distinguished service. He has taken part in the wars of' 62, 65 and 71, and was involved in counter insurgency operations in Nagaland and Manipur. Lt Gen Shankar's last appointment was the Director General of Artillery, during which he oversaw the employment of artillery during the Kargil War. For his distinguished services he has been awarded the Param Vashist Sewa, the Ati Vashist Sewa and the Vashist Sewa Medals.

Dr Skandarbek Ayazbekov

He is the Vice President of the Military Strategic Studies Center under the Ministry of Defence of the Republic of Kazakhstan.

As a legislator, his field is orientalist-cultural studies specialist and fine art expert. He has done Ph.D. and is professor in Art history. He worked in the National Academy of Science and Committee of national Security of the Republic of Kazakhstan.

His field of research is theory and history of civilizations, modern aspects of globalization of international afairs, geopolitical trends of new world order, military and national security, as well as current issues of state development, economics, social, cultural and humanitarian development of the Republic of Kazakhstan.

Ambassador Berdiniyazov Sapar

After finishing secondary school, in 1965 he graduated from Turkmen State University Magtumguly.

He started his working career in 1965 as a teacher of English language in secondary school and then as a staff member of Scientific Research Institute "Luch".

| 1976 | – | Joined Foreign Ministry of Turkmenistan, Ashgabat. |
| 1977 | – | Attache of Consular Department, USSR Ministry of Foreign Affairs. |

1977-1983	–	Attache; USSR Consulate General in Pakistan (Karachi).
1984-1985	–	Senior officer, Ministry of Foreign Affairs of Turkmenistan.
1986-1989	–	Second Secretary, USSR Embassy in Afghanistan (Kabul).
1989-1990	–	Assistant to the Director General of "Turkmenintorg", Ashgabat.
1990-1995	–	Head of the Department; Political Counsellor to the Minister of Foreign Affairs of Turkmenistan.
1995-2012	–	Extraordinary and Plenipotentiary Ambassador of Turkmenistan to the Islamic Republic of Pakistan (Islamabad).
From July 2012	–	Counsellor, Asia and Pacific Department Ministry of Foreign Affairs of Turkmenistan.

Ms Zamira Muratalieva

She is presently Scientific Secretary of the Institute for Strategic Analysis and Prognosis at the Kyrgyz-Russian Slavic University. Her nature of job includes general guidance on the timely and quality execution of scientific researches, organization and preparation of scientific and other reports of the Institute and preparation of proposals for training and development of scientific personnel.

Shri Phunchuk Stobdan (Retd)

Ambassador Phunchuk Stobdan is a distinguished academician, diplomat, author and national security expert. He is a specialist on Asian affairs covering Central Asia and Inner Asia, including Xinjiang, Tibet, Myanmar and the Himalayan region. He has written extensively on a wide range of security-related subjects in a number of professional journals on strategic affairs, books and newspapers, both in India and abroad. He served in Central Asia twice once, as Director at the Embassy of India, Almaty (1999 and 2002) and second time as Ambassador at the Embassy of India, Bishkek (2010-2012). He has also served as Joint Director in the Indian National Security Council. Between October 2006 and November 2007, he was Director of the Centre for Strategic and Regional Studies at the University of Jammu. He is a member of the India International Centre, New Delhi.

Professor Nirmala Joshi

Professor Nirmala Joshi is Research Advisor at the USI. She is a former Head of the Department of Centre for Russian and Central Asian Studies at School of International Studies, Jawaharlal Nehru University, New Delhi. She has been Director, India-Central Asia Foundation, New Delhi and has done various assignments related to Russia and Central Asian studies. She has edited scores of books on India and Central Asia.

Mr Yuriy Makubayev

Mr Yuriy is a scholar at Military Strategic Studies Center (MSSC) of Republic of Kazakhstan. He is currently the Chief Editor of **'Informational and Analytical Journal'**. He is also a member of the editorial board of the Journal **"Defence News"**. He got his Master's degree of Humanitarian Sciences in International Relations from LN Gumilyov Eurasian National University.

Other Participants

1. Mr Aziz Vasikovich Rasulov, Uzbekistan.

2. Ambassador Parakhat H. Durdyev, Turkmenistan.

3. Mr Evgeny Kablukov, Kyrgyzstan.

WELCOME REMARKS

Lieutenant General PK Singh, PVSM, AVSM (Retd)
Director, United Service Institution of India

It is indeed a privilege to welcome you all to this two day international seminar that we are hosting on Central Asia. The United Service Institution of India has had bilateral linkages with Institutes of the Central Asian Republics and we do meet them on a yearly basis. We also meet delegations coming from these countries when they visit Delhi. However, this is the first time we are organizing a seminar in which we are having participants from all the Central Asian Republics, as well as our Indian friends over here.

It is not that the need for a dialogue was not felt, it is also not that the need for mutual interaction with the Central Asian people on a common platform was not felt, but it is just that we were not able to fulfill them together earlier.

I think in today's world there is need to lay emphasis or importance on global linkages of common interests and shared values between our countries. We do realize that each of our countries will have its own national interests, it will also have its own regional interests, and it will also have its own view of international global interests.

But despite all this, I am equally certain that we have a large amount of shared interests in values, shared interests in development of our countries and the region and shared interests in people's prosperity. The challenges that are being faced by the countries of the Central Asian Republics are the challenges that we have either faced or are still facing. There is a lot to learn from each other and a lot to share.

The dynamics of our region, when I say our region, I mean the area from India to Central Asia and the countries in between. There is a lot going to change in the coming years and we have to be prepared for these changes; changes not just in the security environment, but changes also in the economic, political and in all spheres of environment. Towards that end we have had this seminar planned. We should share our views openly, frankly and freely, and increase our contacts, increase our linkages between institutions and our countries.

I will not say anything more. I will now hand over to Sandeep Dewan to carry forward the proceedings. I will only say to our distinguished guests who have come here from these countries that I hope you have a comfortable stay, that you enjoy your time in my country. I hope you make new friends, and go back richer with experience and I am sure we will benefit immensely.

KEY NOTE ADDRESS

Shri Sanjay Singh, Secretary (EAST), MEA

I am honoured to be present before this august audience and speak on a subject which has been the focus of attention of the Ministry of External Affairs over the past two years that is – Enhancing India's Engagement with Central Asia.

Indian engagement with Central Asia is not recent. Relations between India and the region can be traced in history to prior to the fabled Silk Route that wound across the region and linked us culturally, spiritually and commercially. During the Soviet time a close relationship was established with the region. Post-1991 with the independence of the Central Asian countries, India was among the first to recognize them and open embassies in each of their capitals.

The growth in trade and investment has not been rapid but the underlying cordiality and support for each other continues unhampered. We have strong political partnerships with all the Central Asian countries. The past two years have witnessed an exchange of high level visits between India and the Central Asian Republics. Our PM visited Kazakhstan, and the leaders of Uzbekistan, Turkmenistan, Kazakhstan and Tajikistan visited India.

Today India's approach to Central Asia is based on a policy of treating the region as our extended neighbourhood. Central Asia for us is of strategic importance. The relations between our people are civilizational in character. We share two major interests with countries of the region – security and counter terrorism on one hand; and mutually beneficial economic interactions including usage of energy and natural resources on the other. Central Asia also provides opportunities for Indian companies to cooperate in the sectors of education, health, banking, pharmaceutical and transport services. We are engaged in developing the region's connectivity infrastructure. Last year, we revitalized the International North-South Transport Corridor and hope to get the gaps in the corridor filled and enhance connectivity from the port of Mumbai across the region to Moscow and further on to Europe. Spurs along the corridor to add further to connectivity are also being explored. In June 2012 our Civil Aviation Ministry announced 14 flights per week for each of the Central Asian Republics. Kazakhstan, Turkmenistan & Uzbekistan have regular flight connectivity with India and soon we expect Tajikistan and Kyrgyzstan to establish air links with India. We hope that these efforts at improving connectivity will help trade, investment and tourism and raise the present level of trade of US$500 million annually with Central Asia to higher levels. In this endeavour, we also propose to liberalize the issue of visas in order to promote business ties and facilitate people to people contacts.

We have proposed a Comprehensive Economic Cooperation Agreement (CECA) with the Customs Union of Russia, Kazakhstan and Belarus to further integrate India into the region's multilateral processes like the Eurasian Economic Community (EEC) and the Customs Union as well as the Shanghai Cooperation Organisation (SCO).

The overall stability and development of the region, that neighbours Afghanistan, is of considerable interest. With this on our minds, we launched a broad-based new "Connect Central Asia" policy in June 2012 at Bishkek, Kyrgyzstan during the first ever India-'Central Asia Dialogue' which is our Track II effort to improve linkages and people-to-people contacts. The Second India-Central Asia Dialogue will be held in Almaty, Kazakhstan this June.

The Connect Central Asia initiative envisages intensified political level exchanges, strengthening of strategic and security cooperation and deepening of economic, cultural, educational and people-to-people contacts. We have some flagship projects on the anvil such as e-networking of the region. Presently, we have set up IT Centres in all the five capitals and through e-networking hope to develop a delivery programme for Tele-medicine and Tele-education. We are also looking at establishing a Central Asia University in

Bishkek and multi-speciality clinics in the region. We have already completed projects for fruit processing, potato processing, the renovation and up gradation of a hydro-electric power plant, setting up a Machine Tool making unit and computerization of post offices. We are also looking at introducing other small developmental projects in the region.

An important facet of our relations with Central Asia is related to hydrocarbon resources. India is one of the largest importers of oil in the world and demand for gas is growing. Indian companies are in active discussions with Kazakhstan, Turkmenistan and Uzbekistan for upstream, midstream and downstream activities in the oil and natural gas sectors. We are a part of the ambitious TAPI pipeline project which would be a first major link between Central Asia and India. An Indian PSU has a stake in the Satpayev oil block in Kazakhstan and we have signed a civilian nuclear agreement in addition to sourcing of uranium with Kazakhstan. You would also recently have seen reports of the possibility of an oil pipeline from Kazakhstan to India.

India has a development partnership programme with all 5 countries in the region. About 400 young professionals and scholars from Central Asia attend various short term courses annually in India. In addition there are a number of Central Asian students studying in India on scholarships and self-financing basis. We are committed to capacity building and human resource development in the region.

We have Cultural Exchange Programmes with these countries and under this framework a large number of cultural activities are organized. We have very active Indian Cultural Centres in Kazakhstan, Tajikistan & Uzbekistan. Indian films companies are also beginning to look at these countries for foreign film locales. This should also encourage more Indian tourists to visit these countries and vice versa. India is one of the biggest markets for outbound travellers estimated at US$21 billion in 2011.

We cooperate on security issues and share concerns over drug-trafficking, fundamentalism and religious extremism. Through the mechanism of Joint Working Groups on Counter Terrorism with Kazakhstan, Tajikistan & Uzbekistan, we regularly meet and share information and concerns on this crucial area. Kazakhstan, Uzbekistan and Tajikistan are India's declared strategic partners in the region.

India believes that geo-politically we are all shareholders in the stability of Afghanistan which is a bridge between Central Asia and South Asia. How the situation evolves in Afghanistan post-2014 will impact directly on the development and stability of the region. The need of the hour calls for common efforts to tackle fundamentalism and terrorism with Central Asia. We have active defence cooperation and a strong training programme for cadets from these countries in our premier defence institutions like National Defence Academy and Indian Military Academy.

Our relationship with the Central Asian countries is based on a unique model of political, economic, cultural and developmental partnership. India stands for a deep, meaningful and sustained engagement with Central Asia. Our policy of Connect Central Asia will be consonant with our overall policy of deepening engagement in Eurasia and building on our traditional relationship with Russia.

I am indeed very glad to see a leading institution like the USI taking keen interest in Central Asia. The suggestions and thoughts that this Seminar will elicit are bound to help policy makers, scholars and experts in formulating a strategy for deepening engagement between India and Central Asia. It will also lead to more contacts and better understanding of prospects and issues before the region.

I congratulate General Gera and all the members who have put their minds and efforts into this conference.

Session I

Chairperson's Opening Remarks

Ambassador Ashok Sajjanhar, IFS (Retd)

We have with us a very distinguished panel of speakers who will be speaking on regional security perspectives. I think this is a subject that is very critical and crucial as we go forward. I am particularly happy that the Inaugural Address and the Key Note Address have both laid the ground for our discussions in this session and for the rest of the seminar.

Without further ado I will request the speakers to give their perspectives on this very important issue. We have Maj Gen BK Sharma, Ambassador Yogendra Kumar and Lt Gen PC Katoch. Their CVs and resume are contained in the programme booklet, so I will not spend much time except to say that all the three speakers are eminently experienced as far as developments in this region are concerned. What I would support with your concurrence is that all the speakers take about thirty to thirty five minutes which means this session will take around one and half hours, that is, till 12 o'clock or so and after that we will have about forty five minutes for discussion and interaction. If that is alright, then I will like to invite Maj Gen Sharma to take the floor and present his paper.

Session I

First Paper

Major General BK Sharma, AVSM, SM (Retd)**

Regional Security Perspectives

Introduction

Geographically, the landlocked Central Asian Region (CAR) enjoyed a connection with Asia, Europe and Middle East. The 19th century well known geographer Halford Mackinder, described Eurasia as the "heartland of history" and he argued that whosoever "controls it would control the world". Subsequently, the known American strategist Zbigniew Brzezinski highlighted the importance of Eurasia in these words, "---ever since the continents started interacting politically, some five hundred years ago, Eurasia has been the center of world power". Geographically, Central Asia (CA) landmass forms the very core of Eurasia.

The CAR has attracted world attention since time immemorial; the Greeks, Arabs, Chinese, Seljuk Turks, Mongols, Timurids (Sunni Muslims of Turko – Mangol Lineage), Shaybani Uzbeks, and many other conquerors used the CA landmass to expand their respective empires. The Shaybanids ruled parts of the region until the Russians, who first arrived in the region in the mid-18th century, finally consolidated their control in the mid-19th century.

During the 19th Century, the geopolitical rivalry in the region between Great Britain and Tsarist Russia had acquired the dimension of a 'Great Game'. Lord Curzon, in 1898 said, "Turkestan, Afghanistan, Transcaspia, Persia – to many these words breathe only a sense of utter remoteness. To me, I confess they are pieces on a chessboard upon which is being played out a game for domination of the world" The outcome of that strategic conflict was emergence of Afghanistan as a buffer state.

The 20th Century again witnessed a virulent form of great-power conflict which led to Soviet invasion of Afghanistan in 1979. The US perceived this military intervention as an attempt by the Soviet Union to dominate the warm-water ports of Arabian Sea in Pakistan and Iran. The result was that the US, Pakistan, Saudi Arabia funded the opponents of Soviet military presence in Afghanistan, and directed asymmetric Jihadi warfare against them. Later the Soviet Union broke up, but eventually led to the emergence of Af-Pak area as the epicenter of international terrorism.

In the present day the regional strategic security calculus is driven by four main drivers that is, the emerging web of strategic transportation corridors, geopolitics of export energy pipelines Jihadi radicalism and military posturing. In the ensuing geopolitical competition in the region, the Central Asian States (CAS) themselves have not remained mute bystanders. The CAS, US, Russia and China are the protagonists and India, Iran, Pakistan, Turkey and European countries are the peripheral players in his competition. The CAS themselves, as mentioned, have skillfully mastered the art of balancing by pursuing a 'Multi-vector Foreign Policy'.

The paper will briefly discuss drivers of regional security scenario in some measure, future prospects, and India's policy orientation towards the region.

Reconfiguration of Strategic Transportation Corridors

In 100 BC, the region owed its pivotal importance to the famous 6,000 km long 'Silk Route', which linked China with imperial Rome and India through Central Asia. The Silk Route was not only a trade and a transit corridor, but with trade came culture, science and centres of scholarly learning. Central Asia was a melting pot of cross fertilisation of faiths and civilizations. Much of the regional syncretic character can be attributed to that phenomenon.

After its incorporation into Tsarist Russia much of the regional transportation infrastructure was oriented towards Russia. However, after 1991 China and the US are seeking a reconfiguration of strategic transport corridors.

China is fast developing a rail–road infrastructure towards Europe from Xinjiang, through Central Asia to Afghanistan, and Iran. What the Chinese call it as the "New Silk Road" or the "Eurasian Corridor". From Lianyungang in China, 11,870 Kms long corridor will connect the Chinese railway network with the network in Kazakhstan-Kyrgyzstan-Uzbekistan and thence via Russia to Europe (Rotterdam). The European corridor will intersect with the international North-South Multi-modal corridor, which will connect India–Iran–Caspian Littorals, CAS, Russia, Ukraine and Belarus. This 16,000 km long corridor is expected to reduce travelling time by 10-12 days and transportation cost by about 20 percent vis-a-vis Suez Canal route. With the completion of this Eurasian corridor, China will have increased land access to South Asia, Middle East and Europe.

China seeks a strategic congruence with the CAS, and Pakistan in its Arabian Sea Corridor Project. China's interest in Gwadar port, Karakoram overland bridge and consequent presence in Northern areas of Pakistan Occupied Kashmir (POK) need to be analysed in this context. Its access to Bandar Abas and Chabahar ports in Iran on one side, and Gwadar and Karachi in Pakistan on the other, with increased footprints in the crucially important Northern Areas, will have major strategic security implications for India. China's illegal occupation of Shaksgam valley in the POK, the Karakoram highway project, its access to Afghanistan and the increased Chinese presence in northern areas and the Siachen issue will have to be analysed in depth and a detailed manner, and its implications for India in holistic manner.

China's illegal occupation of Shaksgam valley in the POK, the Karakoram highway project, its access to Afghanistan and the increased Chinese presence in northern areas and the Siachen issue will have to be analysed in depth and in a detailed manner, and an assessment of its implications for India.

Former US Secretary Of State Hillary Clinton's articulation of "New Silk Road concept" strategy envisages a reconfiguration of strategic transportation corridor from Central Asia to South Asia via Afghanistan, what they call as the "Corridor of Reforms" much against the interests of China, Russia and Iran. Considering the fragile security scenario in the region this concept for the time being looks far-fetched.

A significant development in the region is - the emergence of Northern Distribution Network (NDN), which is being extensively, used by the US and the North Atlantic Treaty Organisation (NATO) forces for their logistics sustenance in Afghanistan. In fact 75 percent of Logistics are being transported on NDN. In the NDN the centrality of Kazakhstan and Uzbekistan & Tajikistan stands out clearly. In fact, 78 percent of the supplies have to be routed through Uzbekistan thus providing it a leverage in realigning its policy on the US and Russia. Whether NDN emerges as a point of convergence between the competing interests of major players needs to be watched.

The emerging strategic transportation corridors are bound to re-shape the geopolitical and economic landscape of the region. It would impact India as it is an important stakeholder. In the short term, we must expand the scope of our engagement with Tajikistan, Uzbekistan and Turkmenistan for accessing Afghanistan to meet the challenge of Taliban controlled Afghanistan scenario. In the mid-term, land connectivity via Iran and Afghanistan to CAR must be negotiated and implemented despite the US opposition.

In the long-term, at the track II level, we must explore the feasibility of connecting to the region by linking Ladakh /HP with the Western highway of China albeit in the overall gambit of our border dispute with China.

Geopolitics of Energy

Experts note that Central Asia has about 4 percent of the world hydrocarbon resources. Kazakhstan is estimated to be in top 10 countries in terms of proven oil reserves and ranks 16th among the oil producing nations. Kashagan oil field in Kazakhstan is the largest outside the Middle East. Turkmenistan has the fifth largest reserves of natural gas. The South Yoloton gas field in Turkmenistan is known to be the largest gas field in the world. Kazakhstan has the second largest uranium reserves and is the largest Uranium producer in the world. Uzbekistan too is known to have huge deposits of gas and uranium. The People's Republic of China (PRC) will become the largest consumer of Uranium by 2030, overtaking the US. In 2011, Kazakhstan agreed to supply 55,000 tons of uranium to China over next 10 years vis a vis 2100 tones to be supplied to India by 2030. India need to brace up to the competition with China for procurement of this invaluable resource for the country's energy security. Therefore, for continued supply of nuclear fuel, stability in Kazakhstan and deepening of strategic relations with that country are paramount.

The region has tremendous hydro-power resources. Tajikistan has the largest hydropower potential in the world and Kyrgyzstan too ranks very high in this resource. The electricity supply from the region can serve the electricity starved countries like Pakistan and India and mitigate energy security dilemmas of the two countries to a large extent.

Geopolitics of energy resources has become a major driver of competition in the region. An editorial in Times of Central Asia aptly highlights the geopolitics of energy, "the New Great Game is all about oil and gas. The imperial soldiers and spies of the bygone era have given way to engineers and deal makers as the States jockey for the lucrative business of building pipelines to tap the vast resources of the landlocked region". Traditionally, the flow of energy resources has been northwards with Russia having a monopoly on the exploration of resources and their transportation to East and Central Europe. Russia uses energy resources as a strategic tool in furtherance of its national interests vis a vis Europe.

The US led West seek reconfiguration of energy pipelines westward by developing a trans - Caspian Pipeline, connecting it with Baku-Tiblisi- Ceyhan (BTC) pipeline and are seeking to operationalise the Nebucco pipeline. However, Russian opposition to these projects is based on the following; lingering legal dispute of delineation of Caspian sea between the five littorals (Iran, Azerbaijan, Russia, Kazakhstan and Turkmenistan), and the risk of environmental degradation of the Caspian Sea. These objections seem to have dampened the prospects of the western initiative. The most feasible gas pipeline project is from Turkmenistan-Iran-Turkey-Europe. This project is however opposed by the US. The dark horse in the race has been China which despite Russia's reluctance has not only operationalised Atsau-Alashknou oil pipeline but has also secured long term gas contracts in Turkmenistan and is refurbishing the pipeline grid in the region.

As per India's Hydrocarbon vision 2025, India's energy import dependence will increase to about 90 percent. Presently, India imports oil and gas from about 25 countries, with 2/3 of requirement being met from the Middle East. Given the situation in Iran and volatile socio- political situation in the Arab world, it is a strategic security imperative for India to diversify its energy needs from alternate sources like Central Asia. To this end, viable security environment in the region is absolute must for sustainable functioning of Turkmenistan - Afghanistan - Pakistan (TAPI) and Iran-Pakistan-India (IPI) pipelines.

Internal Security

Tajikistan, Kyrgyzstan and Uzbekistan are very low in the markers such as human resource development; widespread corruption and so on. The fragile security situation in Xinjiang, Iran and the Caucasus directly impacts the security scenarios in CAS. The internal ethnic and water disputes and uncertainties of power transitions make the region vulnerable to import of Jihadi terrorism and associated non-traditional military threats.

Ethnic Strife

In Central Asia the ethnic discord is very strong and all the five CAS face this challenge. However, it is most prominent in Kyrgyzstan, Tajikistan and Uzbekistan –located in the Fergana Valley. Kyrgyzstan is faced with a North-South ethnic divide. Northern part is inhabited by ethnic Kyrgyz who have traditionally resisted more conservative Muslim doctrines and practices while the South has large Uzbek population that has for centuries followed more strict interpretation of Islam. This discord can be attributed to the fact that the northerners were nomadic people, while the southerners the Uzbeks were settled people engaged in trade and agriculture. Southern Kyrgyzstan witnessed riots in 1990 and 2010 in which several hundred people were killed and thousands fled to Uzbekistan.

In the Sughd region of Tajikistan bordering Uzbekistan slightly more than 15 percent population is ethnic Uzbeks. The ethnic discord here is between the Tajiks and the Uzbeks. In the mountain settlements of Gorno-Badakshan many smaller groups speak Pamirian languages that are distinct from Tajik, and a significant number of people are Ismailia Muslims who recognise Aga Khan as their spiritual leader. Coupled with extreme poverty and economic hardships, these divisions create a volatile socio-political environment which could be exploited by Jihadis to their advantage.

Water Conflicts

Tajikistan and Kyrgyzstan are upstream countries having control of headwaters of many fresh water rivers particularly the Amu Darya and the Syr Darya to the remainder three countries. Cotton crop and agriculture in downstream countries are dependent of these rivers. Uzbekistan has severely criticized Kyrgyz attempts to build mega hydropower projects as it will affect the flow of the water needed for people's livelihood. Consequently it could have a catastrophic effect on the lives of millions of people who live down stream. Kyrgyzstan and Tajikistan are economically fragile, electricity and energy starved countries. They are dependent on Uzbekistan gas. Attempts by the upper riparian states to affect the flow of water are met with retaliatory steps by Uzbekistan by cutting off electricity gas supply to these countries particularly during harsh winters. Therefore, water has emerged as a potential flash point of conflict in the region.

Regime Transition

After the break-up of the Soviet Union in 1991 there was an outbreak of a civil war in Tajikistan (1992). Kyrgyzstan witnessed 'Tulip' revolution in 2005 forcing the then President Akayev to flee to Russia. Since then the country has experienced instability. Is an 'Arab Spring' or another colour revolution is waiting to happen in Kyrgyzstan? And, if yes, will it have a domino effect on other CAS? Even though the regimes espouse doctrine of Gradualism or Regulated Democracy, there is no Opposition party nor is there any grooming of successors on institution building. On the contrary, patronage network and personal loyalty to the ruler is a rule than an exception. Therefore, transition of regimes remains a critical uncertainty with potential for social unrest and mass uprising. What is worrisome is that in the absence of viable and legitimate political alternatives, the vacuum could be filled by radical elements.

Jihadi Radicalism

The major challenge faced by the CAS is from Jihadi resurgence located in the border lands between Afghanistan and Pakistan known as the Af-Pak region, Turkmenistan, Uzbekistan and Tajikistan share porous & rugged border with Afghanistan and are vulnerable to jihadi threats. During the Taliban regime in Afghanistan, there was spurt of militant activities in the Fergana Valley. This sub- region has a history of Islamic militancy since the Soviet era during when the Basmachi movement had resisted communist control over their way of life. In the post break-up of the Soviet Union the Islamic Renaissance Party was involved in conflict with the communists in Tajikistan civil war. The conflict resulted in a death of more than 50,000 people and nearly 100,000 people became refugees. In the early nineties during the Taliban rule the Islamic Movement of Uzbekistan (IMU) sprang up with Juma Namangami, a veteran of Soviet Army in Afghanistan and Tahir Yuldoshov, an Islamic ideologue, as the leaders who raised IMU with the aim of ousting Islam Karimov and establishing a Caliphate in the country.

During the year 1999, IMU carried out series of bombings in Tashkent. In 2000, they made deep incursions from their bases in Northern Afghanistan, where they were supported by then Taliban regime, to Batken region of Kyrgyzstan and into the Ferghna Valley. They had seized many villages, taken hostages and extorted ransom. Military forces of Kyrgyzstan and Uzbekistan found it difficult to control the situation. In fact, Airforce of Uzbekistan had to launch air strikes inside the territory of Kyrgyzstan to contain these incursions. Post 6/ 11, several hundred of IMU cadres fought alongside Taliban against the Northen Alliance. Juma Namangani was killed in Mazare e Sharif in 2001 and Tahir Yaldosh was killed in South Waziristan in a US drone attack in Aug 2009. The IMU cadres were also involved in serial bomb attacks in Tashkent in 2004.

Presently, cadres of IMU are active in the AF-Pak region. Recently, some new groups namely Uzbek, Islamic, Jihad and Jund-Al-Khalifa. (Soldiers of Jihad) have appeared on the scene and are active in Tajikistan and Kazakhstan.

The Hizb Ut Tehrir (HuT) a pan-Islamic group is also active in the region. This organisation seeks resurrection of Caliphate purportedly by non - violent means. Although the organistaion is not averse to violent methods. The organisation is secretive in nature and has reportedly infiltrated government ranks and wields considerable influence in Fargana Valley.

Approximately 300,000 Uighurs live in Central Asia and are known to be sympathetic to sub- national movement in Xinjiang province. Cadres of East Turkestan Islamic Movement (ETIM), active in Xinjiang, and Chechen extremists, active in the Caucasus, are known to transit through Central Asia to their bases in Afghanistan and frontier areas of Pakistan.

With resurgence of Taliban in Afghanistan, and likely to increase after 2014 the Jihadi network in Central Asia is bound to energise and they are likely to target conveys along the NDN as also the energy infrastructure. Another outcome of Taliban rise will be the armed resistance offered by the Northern Alliance from their bases on Afghanistan border. Nearly 50 per cent of 28 Million population of Afghanistan is Non-Pushtun, concentratated in regions bordering Central Asia and Iran ie, Tajik 25 per cent, Hazaras 19 per cent, Uzbek 6 per cent).

Narco-Terrorism and Drug Trafficking

One of the drug trafficking routes emanating from Afghanistan transverses through Central Asia, Russia, Bulgaria and Eastern Europe. Narco-terrorism is a live problem in the region. It is widely recognized that drug smuggling is closely linked to insurgency, particularly the financial support that sustains it. It also spreads corruption among warlords and sometimes even government officials. Moreover, smuggling routes are often used not just for drugs, but also for bringing terrorists across borders. Tajik authorities had stated that they perceive drugs a more serious threat to their national security than Islamist militancy. Tajik authorities claim that they are responsible for intercepting 85 per cent of the consignment, whereas, as per the world monitors it is merely 10 per cent of the volume that actually transits through the region. The drug addiction by youth and consequent increase in HIV infection is sapping the young population and filling coffers of Jihadi network.

Proliferation of Fissile Material

CAS inherited elements of the vast Soviet weapons of mass destruction (WMD) production complex. Among the activities in which WMD facilities in Central Asia were engaged were uranium mining, plutonium production, the fabrication and testing of biological and chemical weapons, and the storage and testing of nuclear weapons. Early international efforts to address this proliferation threat emphasized ensuring that the Russian Federation became the only legatee of Soviet nuclear weapons; other proliferation risks posed by WMD materials, technology and expertise received less attention. Materials that currently pose WMD-related threats in Central Asia can be classified into three main groups: nuclear weapon-related material, including fissile material (highly enriched uranium and plutonium) and radioactive material (orphan, or abandoned sources); biological weapon-related materials and technologies; and chemical weapon-related materials and technologies. The leading WMD-related risk in Central Asia is the possibility of the theft of materials and their sale by smugglers or through brokers to terrorist or proliferant states. Another risk is the leakage of expertise either through the sale of critical information or through brain drain. A related risk is the possibility that CAS could be used as a transit corridor for smuggling WMD-related materials and expertise originating from outside of the region.

These developments will not augur well for peace and prosperity in the region. Particularly vulnerable to social unrest and Jihadi influence are the areas adjacent to Gorno – Badakshan in Tajikistan and Fergana Valley, the very heartland of Central Asia. The regional countries in general and CAS in particular have to adopt a common approach to prevent internal conflicts and stabilise Fergana Valley.

Militarisation of the Region

The region houses military facilities of Russia, the US and some other countries. Russian facilities include Baikanour Cosmodrome and Anti-Ballistic Missile range in Sary Shagan in Kazakhstan. Kant airbase and a Torpedo testing facility in Kyrgyzstan and a likely military base in the near future in Osh. In Tajikistan, Russia has an airbase at Ayni, a space monitoring station and deployment of 201 Motorised division. The US has a military base in Manas (Kyrgyzstan) and has strong interest in reoccupying Karsi-Khanabad airbase in Uzbekistan. The US is also eyeing air bases in Turkmenistan and Tajikistan. Germany has air force presence in Termez in Uzbekistan and France in Dushanbe. China and Russia are known to have used a "Carrot and Stick" Policy on Kyrgyzstan urging that country to ask Americans to vacate Manas airbase. India has refurbished an airbase in Tajikistan as also set-up a military hospital in that country.

The NATO, the Collective Security Treaty Organisation (CSTO) and the Shanghai Cooperation Organisation (SCO) are the security organisations operating in the region. NATO under its Programme for Peace (PFP) conducts training for the security forces in disaster management, combating drug trafficking, terrorism and proliferation of fissile material. The SCO, on the other hand, has established "Regional Anti-terrorist Centre" at Tashkent and conducts large scale "Peace Mission" series of military exercises biennially. The most active security organisation in the region is Russia led CSTO. It has established a "Regional Anti-Terrorist Centre" at Bishkek, raised a Collective Rapid Reaction Force and conducts annual military training exercises named "Southern Shield".

Future Prospects

American strategic analyst, Owen Lattimore, aptly describes the strategic importance of the region in these words, "the world's new center of_gravity was to be found within a 1000 nm radius drawn around Urumqi, the capital of Xinjiang. This area represented "a whirlpool in which meet the political currents flowing from China, Russia, India and the Muslim Middle East. It encloses more different kinds of frontiers than could be found in any area of equal size anywhere else in the world........".

Seen in the Context of aforesaid statement, the dynamics of great power competition are characterized by a mix of elements of competition, cooperation and conflict. Restoration of Security in Afghanistan and fight against non- traditional threats such as Jihadi network, narco- terrorism, and proliferation of fissile material remain area of common concern and potential cooperation between SCO, CSTO and NATO even though these organizations will remain fundamentally competitive. The main area of competition will be the CAS energy resources and their transportation along divergent routes. Expansion of NATO, overt attempts to establish military bases in the region and deploy Ballistic Missile Defence in Eastern Europe are perceived as harbingers of conflict.

In the short to medium term, China and Russia will remain tactically aligned to each other to counter the US moves under the aegis of CSTO and SCO. However, from long term strategic perspective Russia and China are geographically destined to balance each other. This fundamental factor will cast its shadow on the future trajectory of SCO and its role in CAR, including Afghanistan. In the ultimate analysis the strategic competition in CAR may not be a zero sum game as none of the protagonists have the leverages and bandwidth for singular strategic domination of the region.

Interestingly, in the ensuing power play stands out the role of CAS themselves. They are not mute Spector's to the ongoing competition and have refined the art of multi- vector foreign policy. Their mantra is no single power should dominate CA. They have learnt to deal with major powers pursuing divergent strategic interests in a geo-strategically important space. Commodification of territory such as leasing of military bases, art of regime survival, favouring of patronage networks by the foreign powers etc in the mid of growing sense of relative deprivation by common people are some of the characteristics that attract attention of analysts of the ongoing geopolitical milieu in the region. Which way will each of the CAS swing is a moot point? Will they continue to be simmering, witnesses to the chaos or progress along the path of guided democracy and how will the external players adapt to these internal dynamics are the issues that need to be watched closely and carefully. More importantly, what will be the scenario in post-2014, Afghanistan. How will CAS and other regional countries respond to the upsurge of Taliban? This should remain the primary focus of our strategic discourse.

Concluding Remarks

The developments in CA impact India's strategic security interests. The scramble for energy resources by China, US, EU and Russia impinge on India's efforts to access Central Asian energy. The congruence of strategic interests of China and Pakistan in the transformation of transportation corridors and providing the CA a gateway to the World is bound to marginalize India's otherwise limited influence in the region. Resurgence of Taliban in Afghanistan will radicalize the region and create a wider arc of instability which will have adverse effect on our national security. The developments in CA are moving at a fast pace. India has a short time window to reassert in the region. It is imperative for India to revamp its policies and programmes and take proactive measures to engage with CA more substantially. Strategic Partnership Agreement with Russia and Afghanistan should be energized for the success of meaningful engagement with CA and relations with Iran should be upgraded to strategic level. These steps are essential to develop direct geographical connectivity with the region for trade and import of energy resources.

India must take a hard look to gauge the aspirations of each CAS and seek congruence of own strategic interests with their aspirations.

Must adopt Pro-active stance to participate in regional organizations and structures, build cooperation on Afghanistan inter alia by evolving regional security and development framework and institution building.

Cooperation must be enhanced in intelligence and satellite imagery sharing, border management, joint counter terrorism training, special forces and mountain warfare training, cyber security and counter drug- trafficking and proliferation programmes. Government of India's role is extremely crucial to create an enabling environment for business houses to seek opportunities and flourish.

India's foreign policy orientation should be smart power driven with an interest based multi-vector foreign policy and subtle alignment with Russia.

Session I

Second Paper

Ambassador Yogendra Kumar, IFS (Retd)

Security Perspectives For Southwest Asia-Central Asian Region

The regional security perspectives for the geographical space covering Pakistan, Af-Pak and Central Asia, are likely to get more complex and fraught with difficult ramifications affecting not just the people in the region but farther beyond. Whilst the attitudes of Afghanistan's immediate neighbours – or the other powers, e.g. US, Russia, China, India etc. – towards its current Government are largely favourable, with Pakistan being an exception, the gyre of instability or systemic fragility has widened much more than 2001 as the situation in its immediate neighbourhood has become more vulnerable to negative internal or external triggers.

What is being euphemistically called the transition is, in fact, a transformative event in the region's history. The key event, in the coming months, is the withdrawal of the US and ISAF troops from Afghanistan; however, about 15–30,000 US soldiers would stay behind, ostensibly, for the training and for counter terrorism/ insurgency purposes and the US will retain a capability to conduct drone attacks in the Af-Pak region. Its implications are, first, that the US will continue to have an important role in the eventual shaping of the political order post-2014, and, second, the severely contractionary effect of the troops' withdrawal on a rather weak Afghan economy. Another important aspect of this transformative process is the election for the President in Afghanistan in 2014 for President Karzai's successor.

During this period, an off-and-on dialogue with Taliban is being conducted by the US and in which Pakistan has a key role as the main interlocutors are based there, in Quetta and North Waziristan. Afghanistan has its own process in the form of High Peace Council.

The law and order situation is, somewhat, better than before the US military surge during Gen. Petraeus' time in late 2009. Yet, it remains quite fragile and the possibility of its fragility increasing further is very real. As far as the US ground operations are concerned, its controversial nature came into focus in early March, 2013 when President Karzai asked the ISAF to withdraw their special operations soldiers from Wardak province; this episode brings in to sharp focus the critical nature of local policing challenges before the central government. The situation, as far as law and order is concerned, remains quite fraught in the eastern and southern Afghanistan, including Kabul, but, disturbingly, terrorist incidents in other parts of Afghanistan, including the north-east, are showing an increasing trend.

Relations between Afghanistan and Pakistan remain quite tense and seriously lacking in trust. The two sides accuse each other, with Afghan accusations being repeated by the US as well, of supporting their respective malcontents. There have been instances of exchange of fire between the troops of the two countries, especially in the border regions of Kunar. It is quite likely that this stand-off between the soldiers would get intertwined with the course of the negotiations for political settlement in Afghanistan as well as with the personal distrust between the two leaderships. This tense relationship is likely to lead, during the post-US troops' withdrawal phase, to serious military confrontations between these two increasingly weakening states which are, also, fighting their own numerous domestic battles; this scenario entails even greater regional instability.

As is evident, the lack of political and security stability in Afghanistan is seen by the Taliban and, indeed, Hikmetyar, as well as their protectors in Pakistan, with a sense of triumphalism as the US is perceived by them of having been ousted from Afghanistan just as the Soviet Union/Russian Federation were earlier. Given the rather episodic manner of Pakistani involvement in the efforts to kick-start negotiations, it can be assumed that that Pakistan leadership, especially the military, expects that they will have stronger cards to play in shaping the future of Afghanistan in the days to come.

They feel that they can, now, push their agenda in Afghanistan since the US dependence on them during their troops' withdrawal is especially heavy; the troops' withdrawal via the 'Northern Route' would be nearly five times costlier.

India-Pakistan security matrix is a huge subject in itself and there is no space here to do justice to it. Suffice to say that there is a deterioration in it as the recent events have shown. The Pakistani triumphalism is bound to have a fall-out on this matrix as well. It is likely that Pakistan would continue to see India as an adversary in Afghanistan and pursue its own peculiar agenda there with redoubled vigour in the immediate future.

Once again, the developments in Afghanistan will turn on the Af-Pak fulcrum as they, indeed, have through the millennia. They are expected to have negative effect on the process of political consolidation in Afghanistan which, especially in its recent history, is already showing signs of ethnic fragmentation and polarisation. It is quite likely that we might see the resurrection of the same political and military line-up which existed before the US-led Operation Enduring Freedom in October 2001. It also presages military mobilisation by the non-Pushtoon ethnic communities *vis-à-vis* the possible growing control of the Pushtoons over the national administration. This would, also, have implications in terms of the concerns of neighbouring countries which might feel that the upsetting of the current ethnic configuration of the political forces in Afghanistan would adversely affect their interests.

However, the break-up of Afghanistan appears to be quite unlikely. Even during the earlier period of contestation for capture of power between rival ethnic factions and with the country's effective partition - as, indeed, was the case in 2001; at no stage was the prospect of formal break-up ever considered by either the Taliban or the component members of the Northern Alliance. Destabilising pressures in Afghanistan might also arise from any US/Israeli action against Iran and instability in Pakistan in the immediate or mediate future.

The regional security perspective needs to take into account a wider dimension. There is also the onset of leadership transition period for Uzbekistan, Kazakhstan and Tajikistan whilst Kyrgyzstan has a government which has not yet achieved consolidation. Disturbingly, in the Central Asian countries, the old malcontents and new radical elements from their own respective countries have found safe havens and the opportunity to train in terrorist activities in Pakistan. These developments are quite evident in Tajikistan, Uzbekistan, Kyrgyzstan and Kazakhstan. According to Jane's Intelligence Review [January, 2012], the Central Asian countries are preparing for renewed security problems post-US withdrawal. Following the Operation Enduring Freedom, various Central Asian militant groups, along with Al Qaeda and the Taliban, escaped to Pakistan's tribal areas. Amongst the existing groups fighting against the Central Asian countries are the Islamic Movement of Uzbekistan (IMU) [active in north-eastern Afghanistan, Tajikistan and southern Kyrgyzstan], its splinter groups called Islamic Jihad Union, the revived United Tajik Opposition [UTO], a new group called Jama'at Ansarullah [active in Tajikistan], Zhayshul Mahdi [active in Kyrgyzstan], another new group called Islamic Movement of Kyrgyzstan trained in Af-Pak area, Jund al-Khalifah based in Af-Pak area [active in Kazakhstan], LashkareTvaiba Kazakhstan [possibly named after the Pakistani group Lashkar-e-Tayyiba] and some odd Kazakh Salafi elements. This report, also, mentions that the reported seizures of Afghan narcotics in Central Asia are several times higher than 10 years ago.

Since July 2010, Russia has been trying to persuade the Tajik government to allow its border guards to help monitor the Tajik-Afghan frontier as they were doing until 2005. Russia has succeeded in getting the lease of Russia's 201st Division in Tajikistan renewed for another 49 years. Russia is also strengthening its base in Kant in Kyrgyzstan and is in talks about establishing another base in the south of the country.

A further ramification is not just in regard to the Central Asian countries but the wider international community. And, that is, in the event of things spinning out of control, Afghanistan and the Af-Pak region could become once again a haven for terrorists of all variety from where operations in different parts of the world could be mounted, as was the case before the US action in 2001 and as it is with other places situated within failed or failing states, such as

Yemen and Mali. Even if there may not be enough physical space for the actual military training for terrorist attacks, Afghanistan and the Af-Pak region would, certainly, become a place from where radical propaganda and drug smuggling would sustain terrorist movements. Moreover, this time the circle of instability with potential spawning of terrorists will be even wider than was the case even in 2001.

Is there a possibility of Afghanistan emerging from this cycle of intra-ethnic conflict and fragmentation, followed by external intervention? One way is to bolster the efforts of the Karzai Government to bring about an all-inclusive administration. How this policy is strengthened to address the governance deficit will have a major impact on the future of Afghanistan. Similarly, pressure needs to be further exerted on Pakistan to ensure that no terrorist attacks are mounted from its territory. Given that the combination of circumstances, today, are more favourable to the Karzai Government unlike the previous regimes, this approach has prospects; yet, fluidity remains and the circumstances, as stated above, can easily get out of control.

As for the way out, one needs to take a leaf out of the history of the Af-Pak region itself. Of the many generals who trod the Af-Pak soil throughout its history, there is one who is never mentioned. Dressed in his loincloth and in leather sandals with his walking staff, Gandhi, during his visit in 1938, toured the region accompanied by his favourite disciple, the Frontier Gandhi. There is a photograph of the Mahatma sitting at a public rally in the company of proud Pushtoons in their tall turbans as Badshah Khan is addressing the gathering; they all present an arresting picture of civilized, quiet dignity so characteristic of the Pushtoons. The latter's now-forgotten organisation, the Khudai Khidmatgar, was an amazing example of non-violent grassroots' political mobilisation against the repressive control of the British Raj. The movement, starting in the late 1920s, was so well organised that, during the 1930 Salt Agitation not only were the volunteers peaceful during the entire agitation but, through their discipline, they rendered the oppressive Raj machinery ineffective. The famous incident of the crack First Garhwal Rifles, the most decorated regiment of the day, refusing their British officer to open fire on the peaceful Khudai Khidmatgars marching on the main road in Peshawar caught the imagination of the people of

India leaving the British completely shaken up. Yet again, during the Quit India Movement, when the British were at their nervous worst at the most difficult time in the Second World War, the city of Peshawar was taken over, without a shot being fired, by them for over a week. This episode is in sharp contrast to the violence and lawlessness in other parts of India; an example is eastern UP and Bihar where the violent uprising against the British led to the collapse of the administration for months. Moreover, the political influence of the Khudai Khidmatgars was such that, at the time of partition, in an instance of the principle of self-determination being put on its head, Badshah Khan asked his followers not to participate in the referendum allowing others to vote in favour of Pakistan. Such a level of mobilisation amongst the Pushtoons is in painful but stunning contrast with the current mayhem, the suicide bombers, the car bomb blasts etc. which are in evidence in the Af-Pak area.

The essential point is that the grassroots' political mobilisation is the best counter to the fragmented and violent politics which is so pervasive in parts of Afghanistan and the Af-Pak. A democratically organised political force, which is non-violent, inclusive and empowering of its grassroots membership, is the only way in which long-term stability can be provided in Afghanistan and Af-Pak. There are ways of achieving that, through political reforms, which will produce enduring social and political stability to effectively counter against radicals of whatever variety as was demonstrated by Badshah Khan. The Pushtoons, like the other traditional societies, have strong democratic tradition of grassroots governance by consent which, through international intervention, has been extinguished repeatedly in the tragic history of Afghanistan; the Soviet occupation and the US military action have meant, as is only natural, the imposition of their own respective political models on a hapless society. This Afghan tradition, despite these experiences, surfaces again and again even in its current history. The source of the turmoil in Afghanistan, as described above, needs to be removed so that the future generations in Afghanistan, and perhaps elsewhere in the region and beyond, are spared the on-going bloodbath which only threatens to get worse in the coming days.

Session I

Third Paper

Lieutenant General PC Katoch, PVSM, UYSM, AVSM, SC (Retd)

Regional Security Perspective: The Role of Major Powers

Introduction

The CARs (CARs) measuring some four million sq km is inhabited by just over 64 million people with most population concentration in the Fergana Valley and its periphery and the north of Kazakhstan. With GDP of USD166 billion, per capita GDP of USD 2,700 billion and being landlocked, access to sea ports range from 2,770 kilometers to 5,500 kms. Another feature of CARs is the expanses of desert the Kara Kum and the Ksyl Kum and mountain ranges; the mighty Tien Shan has led to vast unpopulated areas lying alongside other relatively densely populated areas. Many are unaware that some of the present day Indian population has its ancestry in CARs, and it is the eastward migration of inhabitants centuries ago, on account of drying up of river basins, that led to founding the Indus Valley Civilization.

For the CARs, unexpected breakdown of USSR did create chaos with territorial disputes erupting overnight, but it also created new opportunities including new partners and allies. The US, Turkey, Iran, India and Pakistan, China and Russia were quick to establish relations with the new countries. What is referred as the 'New Great Game' today, actually is the modern version of the traditional power plays in the region by the major players (Russia, China, the US) due to the increasing importance of Central Asia stemming from existence of vast reserves of hydrocarbons (oil and gas) and minerals like uranium, and its geopolitical location in the centre of Eurasia as well as its strategic position as a link between major markets of Europe and Asia. The region is inexorably linked to Afghanistan with growing uncertainties of post 2014. A regional security perspective must include internal dynamics of CARs and the inter pay of external factors. The security paradigm in Central Asia is often not regionally interrelated and interdependent but rather influenced by external powers on an individual state-unit rather than regional level, multilateral security frameworks, notwithstanding. CARs have differing attitudes towards external attempts to influence regional politics and security. For example, 80 percent of US investment in CAR is in Kazakhstan, which is perhaps not liked by some other CAR countries. It would not be wrong to say that Uzbekistan and Turkmenistan regard US influence in the region as a challenge in itself. Therefore, CARs can be expected to respond at different levels to foreign military presence despite possibility of increased Taliban influence in Afghanistan.

Internal Dynamics

A transition economy, unemployment, drug trade, illicit weapons are factors that contribute to instability in any country coupled with lack of governance, inept handling of social change, lack of avenues of political expression and justice. Central Asia is an area offering certain geo-economics advantages to countries or multinational corporations that have particular regional or global aspirations, due either to their own interests or to the need to neutralize other nations or companies which they see as rivals. As per the International Monetary Fund (IMF), in Caucasus and Central Asia, the economic outlook remains favorable, reflecting high oil prices that are benefiting oil and gas exporters, supportive commodity prices and remittance inflows benefiting oil and gas importers, and, for both groups, moderate direct exposure to Europe. The positive outlook provides an opportunity to strengthen policy buffers to prepare for any downside risks. However, the outlook on unemployment, drugs and illegal weapons is not that bright. The economic crisis has caused millions of migrant labourers from Tajikistan, Kyrgyzstan and Uzbekistan to lose their jobs in the boom economies of Russia and Kazakhstan. Unemployment rates in Kazakhstan, Kyrgyzstan and Uzbekistan are 6.1 percent, 8.2 percent and 8 percent respectively, which are manageable. However, Tajikistan and Turkmenistan have unemployment rates of 60 percent and 70 percent respectively; Afghanistan's unemployment rate comparatively is only that of 36 percent. Such a situation leads to instability and is conducive to terrorism, especially since this large unemployed segment has access to vast quantities of drugs from both Afghanistan and Iran. This segment is lured into this nefarious trade and easily become conduits for drug trafficking. In 2009 itself, some 90 metric tons of drugs came from Afghanistan. Then is the problem of illegal weapons which has alarmed most CARs and seizures by security forces has taken place in Tajikistan, Kyrgyzstan, Kazakhstan and Uzbekistan. Gun running in CARs is endemic with illegal weapons coming from Russia, China, Iran and Pakistan, latter via Afghanistan. In June 2012, Kyrgyzstan admitted that only half of the small arms that went missing during the country's 2010 political and ethnic violence have been accounted for and the missing quantities are considered enough to carry out another revolution.

Another important factor contributing to instability and insecurity in the CAR is border disputes. For example, borders among Kyrgyzstan, Uzbekistan and Tajikistan are not properly defined. Fergana Valley is rife with territorial disputes, especially in densely populated areas with competition for resources and friction periodically erupts into violence among Kyrgyz, Tajiks and Uzbeks. Earlier these borders were drawn on an irrational basis by the Soviet Union and subsequently became borders between sovereign states. The Fergana Valley is also teeming with various extremist / terrorist elements and their engaging in larger conflicts cannot be discounted. There has also been problem of rivalry like between Uzbekistan and Kazakhstan. Serious ethnic divisions like in Kyrgyzstan in June 2010 caused hundreds, mostly Uzbeks, killed and over 2000 homes and buildings destroyed. There is also the risk that Central Asian *jihadis* currently fighting alongside Taliban in Afghanistan may take their struggle back home after 2014. This would increase instability and pose major difficulties for Central Asia and even China. Tajikistan already faces a threat from the Islamic Movement of Uzbekistan (IMU), a group with a vision of an Islamist caliphate that is fighting in Afghanistan alongside the Taliban.

External Factors

There is no denying that US and China are rivals in competing for the untapped mineral wealth and hydrocarbons straddling the vast expanse from the Xinjiang-Kazakh/Kyrgyz border to the western shores of the Caspian Sea. In pursuit of their multivector foreign policy the CARs have   individual perceptions on how best their political and economic interests can be served which differs vastly.

USA. At the Istanbul Conference on Afghanistan, in November 2011 Hillary Clinton, then Secretary of State had articulated the concept of New Silk Road Strategy as "a web of economic and transit connections that will bind a region too long torn apart by conflict and division." The US perceives Central Asia, South Asia and Southeast Asia as a region playing a crucial role in stabilizing Asia, with Afghanistan as the land bridge between CAR and Eurasia and South-Southeast Asia. However, the key problems are the outright refusal by Pakistan to provide access to Afghanistan by land to India and the US-Iran tensions on the nuclear issue have reduced the option of reaching out to Afghanistan and the CARs vis-a-vis its territory. Resultantly, both the Turkmenistan-Afghanistan-Pakistan-India (TAPI) and the Iran-Pakistan-India (IPI) pipelines have not been realized yet. As of now, India's access to CARs is through the Iranian port of Chahbahar.

China. China has made enormous investments in CARs; Kazakh and Uzbek oil, Turkmen gas and Kyrgyz and Tajik mineral wealth. Her geographical proximity is of enormous advantage. China already has trade with CAR to the tune of $ 29 billion as compared to just $500m in case of India. China also has stakes in Iranian energy resources, for which, she would like to make use of the Iran-Turkmenistan cooperation for oil and gas exploration. This link once established and made functional would help China flood the Central Asian markets with its goods. China has also invested in Afghanistan including building a railroad from Logar to Kabul and China's Chinese National Petroleum Corporation (CNPC) began Afghan oil production in October 2012, with extracting 1.5 million barrels of oil annually. China has an active plan for a quadrilateral freight railroad from Xinjiang through Tajikistan, Afghanistan to Pakistan. The ultimate destination for China's Silk Road politics is

Eurasia across Central Asian Steppes or the heartland of the Turkic region and the former Eastern Europe. China envisages rail, road and oil/gas pipelines through this heartland and numerous arteries feeding it from south and finally landing in the European Continent. China's CNPC built a pipeline connecting China's eastern coast with gas fields of Turkmenistan in just 18 months in 2007-2008 and is extending it to reach the Caspian Sea. The CNPC plans to expand its natural gas network to other Central Asian states and Afghanistan in the next five years. China has also taken on the region's highway, railroad and electricity transmission challenges through very difficult terrain for Chinese goods to reach Europe, the Middle East and Chinese-built ports in Pakistan and Iran. But there are downsides to the China-CAR relationship with growing belief of economic hegemony laced with negative images of environmental depredation by Chinese mines, bad working conditions in Chinese plants, and Chinese businessmen squeezing out competitors with liberal bribes to officials. The nationalist sentiment in the region also views with suspicion Chinese demographic invasion including illegal immigrants. Beijing is starting to take tentative political and security initiatives in the region through Shanghai Cooperation Organisation (SCO) but this organization has proved ineffective in times of unrest. Beijing's major concern also is the security and development of its Xinjiang Autonomous Region, which shares 2,800 kilometers km of borders with Kazakhstan, Kyrgyzstan and Tajikistan. The core of its strategy seems to be creation of close ties between Xinjiang and Central Asia, with the aim of reinforcing both economic development and political stability. China has been engaging Taliban to induce them to scale back their perceived support for Uighur separatist groups, such as the East Turkestan Islamic Movement (ETIM). Yet, Chinese policy makers have yet to come up with a clear plan to work toward stability in both Afghanistan and Central Asia while ruling out any military intervention even in a case of extreme unrest. But, if Chinese investments and national interests are threatened, they may force to do so. On balance, China's CARs policy rests on four objectives; keeping Uighur separatists down, keeping northeastern neighbors stable, managing natural resources effectively and continuing to develop new markets.

Russia - Russia is determined to maintain interests and access in Central Asia by dominating the security framework through Collective Security Treaty Organisation (CSTO) and controlling major pipelines that allow resources to enter and exit the region. In addition to economic, labor and stability interests, Russian interests also lie with the large Russian populations in Kazakhstan and Turkmenistan. More recently, Russia is attempting to integrate CARs into the Eurasian Union that creates a dilemma for the countries in the region albeit Kazakhstan seems to have decided to join. Whether CARs Kyrgyzstan and Kazakhstan in particular, will join Russia's Eurasian Union or tilt to China is the test for Russian influence in the region. Eurasian Union would have negative effect on investment China has made on both sides of its border. Erection of a Russia controlled tariff barriers will adversely affect China's trade with CARs.

Iran - Iran has already invested 340 million US dollars in the development of Chahbahar port and India's contribution is over 100 million dollars. At the same time India has invested over 136 million dollars in the construction of Afghan Ring Road Highway (Helmand sector) that will be connecting Chahbahar with Kabul and thus provide Kabul access to Indian Ocean. This fits with the Russian concept of constructing North-South corridors. Denied land access through Pakistan, this is the avenue for India to connect with Central Asia. Iran is eager to develop her eastern region and expand her trade with Afghanistan and Central Asia, and is also working to link Mashshad with Herat in Afghanistan. The Chahbahar-Kabul link for trade and commerce will enable oil and gas rich Central Asian states of Kazakhstan, Uzbekistan and Turkmenistan to reach the South East and South Asian markets. This route will also suit western nations in addition to via Caspian Sea.

Regional Security Paradigm

In view of the above mentioned regional security scenario and the role of major and regional power, the problems/threats can be summarized as:

   (a) Centrifugal forces within Central Asia causing disparity, rivalry and lack of trust.

(b) Weak economy, political systems and corruption.

(c) Security crisis; border and ethnic conflicts, drug trafficking and the rise of religious extremism.

(d) The nature of threat in the region in the post 2014 scenario.

(e) The nature of emerging competition between US, China, Russia in the region. Will it remain benign or get into conflict? The ability of regional groupings such as the CSTO, and SCO promoting geopolitical ambitions

(f) And increasing PLA capacity and modernization and its likely impact on regional security.

Regional Security Architecture

The security interdependence between states in the region is particularly intense because of the nature of perceived security threats. These threats are transnational non-traditional security threats in nature and dominate the Central Asian security narrative, implying these have an extensive impact on the region and require a regional response but regional security dynamics are defined by mutual suspicion. Over the past few years, SCO and CSTO appear to be staking out complementary, rather than competing, mandates. There appears to be under-the-surface competition between the two groups. The new International Crisis Group (ICG) writes in its report titled "China's Central Asian Problem" that Russia continues to seek military influence in Central Asia but has become increasingly distrustful of the SCO and Chinese intentions. It also notes that China has not been able to match its ambitious economic moves with political and military muscle because of strong Russian influence in CARs security structures. Russia continues its monopoly of arms sales to CARs. Therefore, relations between CSTO and SCO remain uncertain and potentially competitive but these organizations have proved ineffective in crisis.ICG assesses that in case of a power vacuum in the region, even if either China or Russia is willing to intervene militarily in Central Asia, China may take the lead. However, this ICG assessment is just one view. Post 2014, there is also good chance of Afghanistan increasingly integrating with SCO assuming greater role in Afghanistan. Simultaneously, there is also possibility of more CSTO-NATO cooperation since China cannot provide security for its investments in the region, particularly Afghanistan, and Russia understands adverse effects of radical dispensation in Kabul.

Conclusion

The regional security perspective in CAR is fluid and has varied possibilities. Finally, the quantum of US troops in Afghanistan post 2014, Pakistan's capacity for mischief, the posture of Taliban, level of instability in Afghanistan and possibility of another international force (like from OIC countries) are a matter of speculation but CARs certainly need to integrate more intimately into the security framework of the region.

Session - I: Discussion

Regional Security Perspectives

Question - How are the dynamics of security and energy going to shape in the Central Asian region?

Response - The linkages between the CARs and their neighbours cannot be wished away. Since independence, the trajectories of the CARs have changed from the predominant Russian influence to the pursuit of independent policies. They are charting new course for themselves, which are based on their national interest. But the regional instability in the region is there to stay and is a cause of concern. Besides, the fear of radicalisation by Al-Qaeda and Taliban is also looming over the CARs.

Security dynamics is extremely fluid in the Central Asian region. Developments in Afghanistan are central to the security environment of the CARs. Thus the developmental needs of the CARs are to be watched very carefully. Keeping in view the energy potential of the region, the involvement of Big Players in the region is inescapable. The trans-Caspian pipeline is not going to fructify because it does not serve the US interest. On the other side, Russia is not happy with the Chinese involvement in the CARs. The future of Turkmenistan-Afghanistan-Pakistan-India (TAPI) and the Iran-Pakistan-India (IPI) is also uncertain because of the instability in Afghanistan and Baluchistan.

China does not want to deploy its armed forces in this region. The Collective Security Treaty Organisation (CSTO) is trying to increase its footprints in the region after "Operation Tulip" (2005). In Afghanistan and Iran things are not planned, they are just happening. Thus the security scenario is fluid in the CARs and Afghanistan. In fact the CARs have not even integrated themselves even after a decade of their independence. Since The Shanghai Cooperation Organisation (SCO) and the CSTO have been ineffective as regional groupings to shape the security of the region, it will continue to remain in a state of flux. Russia and China are trying to spread their influence in the region independently rather than collectively. Russia has countered the SCO by proposing the Eurasian Union. Now the dilemma for the CARs is to select between SCO and Eurasian Union. But whatever be the case, the solutions will come from only the CARs.

Question - The CARs are the focal point for India in the region. India has role in South Asia and West Asia. How does India plan to play its role in CARs?

Response - India has a definite place in CAR region which cannot be taken away by China or any other nation. It is thus espousing a new policy "Connect Central Asia Policy "for the CARs by encouraging investment in the region by Indian Public Sector Undertakings (PSUs). But the biggest problem is of connectivity to the region. Frantic efforts are on to work out options to ensure connectivity to CARs through Iran, which will ensure increase in engagement with the region. The increased connectivity will change the perspective of CARs towards India, which will find a prominent place in the development process of CARs.

India's Connect Central Asia Policy can be a mirror image of India's "Look East Policy", which has done well for both India and the South Asian nations. India thus needs to increase its presence in the region. This may include exchange of scholars, academicians and Defence personnel. A good beginning has been done by opening a Central University at Bishkek, a centre for e-education and tele-medicine. This will ensure that Indian presence in the region will provide a big impetus to economic activity and eventually develop into a comprehensive strategic and economic relationship with these states.

Like India, CARs are also multi-cultural and multi-ethnic, hence their interests are similar. Thus they can emulate Indian experience for inclusive growth and development.

Question - Is there any concrete strategy of India for CARs?

Response - India is at a disadvantageous position, as it does not share boundary with any of the CARs unlike Pakistan, China and Iran, the other influential players in the region. Thus India's strategy towards CARs has traditionally been that as "soft power". This indeed can be utilized effectively to engage these nations towards their cultural and economic development. In fact the prevalent diversities of India will be handy in engaging the CARs. Even the cultural connections of India with the CARs are linkages for present engagement. The Indian strength lies in its knowledge of the Information Technology sector which can contribute in a big way in building up economic relations between CARs and India.

Thus the Indian strategy towards CAR should be governed by the following factors:-

- The past historical contacts and cultural linkages can become a bridge in the present.

- People to people contacts should be encouraged.

- The CARs Head of states had lot of expectations from India, as a result, after independence India was among the first few countries they visited for engagement. But unfortunately India could not capitalize on the situation because of poor economic conditions prevailing in the country.

- India can play a role of a 'balancer' in the region, but lack of connectivity has proved to be a big hindrance.

- Indo-CARs relations are to be looked at from the following as well:

  - The commonality of building a democratic and liberal polity with market oriented economy.

  - Self-sustainability.

  - Capacity building in security, strategic, military economic skills etc.

Question - Steel Authority of India Ltd (SAIL) has contracts for exploration of iron ore and the Oil and Natural Gas Corporation (ONGC) for oil and gas in CARs What will be the impact of this co-operation in view of Taliban making inroads into CARs?

Response - Security of the Indian projects in CARs is a problem. Without adequate security on the ground, it would be difficult for these the projects to fructify. Once Taliban finds it way in CARs, these projects would further face the heat and may close down.

Question - Is the presence of US and NATO in CARs a part of the problem? Will India's engagement with CARs be best achieved through Iranian route?

Response - The US and The North Atlantic Treaty Organisation (NATO) presence in CARs is not a problem, in fact it has provided these nations a stability and immunity from Taliban. However the problem may get acute in the post 2014 withdrawal of these forces when the real impact of Taliban will be visible. The CARs are thus as of now happy with the US presence in the region. However, of late the US sensitivity is not in tune with the sensitivity of the region for which the CARs are unhappy and the situation is a cause of concern for them. But they still would like a token presence of the US forces to cater for the post 2014 scenario.

The Indian connectivity to CARs through the Chabahar route in Iran can be a 'game changer. Hence the MEA should consider this as a policy instrument. This route will be a great balancing factor for the connectivity with CARs, in fact, could prove to be a Gwadar equivalent to India.

Question - In the context of CARs, instead of India's soft power, is there any other methodology of engagement?

Question - Since the SCO has been ineffective, what is its future? What is the relevance of CICA?

Response - The CARs are a big source of energy and gas, hence have espoused great interest with the Big Players and their involvement. Though SCO's role is diminishing in the region, yet it wants to create an 'energy club'. But Russia is seeking to limit Chinese involvement in the region and thus is aspiring for a lead role in the region by countering the Chinese inroads in the CARs by proposing the idea of a Eurasian Union for the region.

SCO and CICA are relevant today and both will shape up on

their own dynamics. India is engaged with SCO and CICA, but it needs to enhance the engagements. As of now India has only an 'observer' status in SCO and is seeking its full membership. But SCO being a China driven organization, it is unlikely that the Indian membership for SCO will be cleared by China soon.

Question - What has been the success of Doha talks on reconciliation? What is its effect on future scenario of Afghanistan?

Response - The 'High Peace Council' has been a non-starter from the very beginning as the Taliban does not recognize the Constitution of Afghanistan. Hence reconciliation is not feasible. India is certainly not going to engage Taliban, as the US could not succeed with its military and economic might.

Question - India has not engaged CARs since their independence. What is the current strategy of engagement with CARs keeping in view India's national interest (primarily energy security)?

Response - India missed the opportunity of engaging with the CARs in the 90's. The Head of states of Uzbekistan, Tajikistan and Kazakhstan visited India after their Independence with lots of hope, but felt neglected by the lack of its involvement. However India's economic problems and difficulties have been addressed and things have improved since then, hence new initiatives can now be taken up as 'India has become a rising power'. The abundant availability of uranium, oil and gas in the CARs has great prospects of trade for India.

However the government of India is encouraging its business leaders and enterprises to take the initiative.

Session II

Chairperson's Opening Remarks

Lieutenant General Vinay Shankar, PVSM, AVSM, VSM (Retd)

I must admit that the morning session was India centric, may be that is how it ought to be. Now our guests have a clear perspective on how India has been looking at its relationship with the Central Asian countries. The views were diverse, yet one could discern a thread which was common to all the speakers and broadly gave substance to the way India is looking at the Central Asian Republics. With that, platform having been set, I must welcome each guest present here. Now we are more balanced, we have just one Indian speaker and we have four speakers from the Central Asian countries. Given the time schedule we will cut down the time a little. We will give twenty minutes to each speaker and the rest of the time for question and answer session.

The broad theme of the seminar must be kept in the background, that is "Enhancing Engagement with the Central Asian Republics". So when we look at the Afghan conundrum and related areas, I am sure these will come up in the presentation. That bigger picture has to be kept in mind. I will not take more time and request the first speaker to make his presentation.

Session II

First Paper

Ambassador Ashok Sajjanhar, IFS (Retd)

The Afghan Conundrum And Regional Approach

The attack on Afghanistan by USA and the North Atlantic Treaty Organisation –International Assistance Force (NATO-ISAF) forces styled as the War on Terror started on the heels of the attacks on the World Trade Centre buildings in New York and the Pentagon in Sept, 2001. Twelve years later the United States and the NATO-ISAF forces appear to be as far if not farther from achieving their original objective of destroying the Taliban and al-Qaeda and making America and the world safe from terrorism.

The two significant achievements that USA can count in its war in Afghanistan over this period are the elimination of Osama bin Laden and also ensuring that no subsequent terrorist attack takes place on the territory of USA. This is of course notwithstanding the large number of terrorist attacks that have shaken and caused immeasurable death and destruction all over the world including in London, Madrid, Bali, Mumbai and many other cities in several countries.

If one looks at the condition of people of Afghanistan, it is a different story with terrorist attacks taking place regularly and frequently on a daily basis resulting in large numbers of casualties and enormous carnage. Moreover America is trying to woo back the same Taliban into Afghanistan which it had thrown out of the country in 2001. USA had come to this region to drive out the Al Qaeda and the Taliban so that Afghanistan would not be a safe haven for terrorists. Today this Region is less stable, harbours more terrorists and presents a greater security threat to the US as well as to the region and the World:

It is unclear how the security situation in Afghanistan and in the neighboring countries will evolve over the next two years and beyond. This will have a profound impact on the security architecture not only of this Region but of whole of Asia and the World. Several differing scenarios are being projected and visualised, some more probable than the others.

Let us start by recounting a few facts.

Firstly, at the international level, there is a sense of fatigue with the unending fighting and elusive peace in the country. The sense of tiredness also envelops the Afghan population both in the South as well as North of the country. The ongoing efforts to muster financial support for sustaining the process of stabilisation of the Afghan state appear to be lackadaisical and half-hearted. At Tokyo, the international community did make a pledge of $16 billion for the next four years, which is much less than what the Afghan President had demanded at Bonn ($10 billion per year) and short of what the Afghan Central Bank estimated ($6-7 billion per year) as necessary for sustaining economic growth. The adverse effects of decreasing international aid on critical areas—related to building democratic institutions, ensuring gender equality and strengthening of the media—have already decelerated the process of stabilisation in Afghanistan.

Secondly, all countries of the region have enormous stakes in the stability and security of Afghanistan. They have all benefitted from the US-NATO led operations in Afghanistan.

However, these countries also have their own interests and agendas. Pakistan is looking for strategic depth; Iran wants to see the back of American forces from Afghan soil as soon as possible; China eyes Afghan resources without any definite commitment to invest in Afghan security and stability; Russia is ready to engage as a service provider if funds can be arranged elsewhere. The Central Asian countries, three of whom border Afghanistan, have their own concerns, anxieties and apprehension regarding the emerging scenario in the country. The willingness of regional actors to play a leading role in stabilising Afghanistan, rather than pursuing divergent national interests and disparate agendas, is also uncertain. Unless the Central Asian states, China, India, Iran, Pakistan and Russia jointly contribute towards ensuring stability, there is considerable possibility that Afghanistan could fall to the Taliban again or even break up with a massive civil war taking a heavy toll.

The several formidable challenges confronting the Government and people of Afghanistan encompass but are not limited to security, countering insurgency, controlling cultivation and trade of narcotics, dealing with corruption, ensuring development etc.

Although expected to be partial, the drawdown by US and NATO forces will leave a significant security deficit in Afghanistan. It is understood that currently there are around 68,000 US and more than 30,000 ISAF troops in Afghanistan, the figure having come down from the 140,000 plus figure which was reached in the middle of 2011 before the drawdown commenced. It is now clear from discussions between Presidents Obama and Karzai as also from the announcements made by the two governments that there are expected to be around 34,000 US troops in Afghanistan by Feb, 2014. It is clear that 2014 will not see a total withdrawal from Kabul but only a drawdown. According to current indications there are expected to be about 10 - 20,000 troops which will be engaged largely in Special Operations, counterterrorism activities and military training programmers.

The Afghan National Security Forces have already started taking over security maintenance operations in different regions of the country. They would be expected to assume total responsibility for ensuring safety and security of the country much before the US and NATO troops leave in 2014.

The willingness of regional actors to play a leading role in stabilising Afghanistan, rather than pursuing divergent national interests and disparate agendas, is also uncertain. Unless the Central Asian states, China, India, Iran, Pakistan and Russia jointly contribute towards ensuring stability, there is considerable possibility that Afghanistan could fall to the Taliban again or even break up with a massive civil war taking a heavy toll.

The US and its allies hope that the peace process, which began nearly two years ago, will gain traction before most international forces withdraw from the country in fewer than 20 months. This however appears highly unlikely as the relationship among the key players - the US, Afghanistan and Pakistan - is marked by distrust that does not allow the rather tentative and uncertain discussions to develop any momentum or substance. Some positive and encouraging statements purportedly emanating from the Taliban leadership do not in any way represent a change of heart on the part of Taliban. This move appears to be purely tactical to lull its opponents into complacency and to create larger political and negotiating space for itself. Talks over the last few months by President Karzai whether in London with PM David Cameron and President Zardari, or in Washington with President Obama have not helped to reduce hostility or suspicion between the different interlocutors.

President Karzai recently warned the West not to use peace talks as a lever against his government. He said that Taliban and US are working together to undermine the credibility of his government.

In the post-2014 scenario, the role of regional countries is likely to increase significantly. The Central Asian states, particularly Tajikistan, Turkmenistan and Uzbekistan, who share borders with Afghanistan, will be directly affected by instability in that country. Due to a persistent inadequacy of state capacity and military capability, these states can at best try to ensure that their territory is not used as safe haven by the Taliban. They could also contribute with limited logistics support.

Out of the three countries, Uzbekistan has the most active and vibrant relations with Afghanistan although it shares only a short 137 km border with that country and there are just 1.5 to 2 million Uzbeks on the Afghan side of the border.

The longest border of 1300 km is with Tajikistan and about 8 million Tajiks live on the Afghan side of the border. Both Tajikistan and Uzbekistan are prone to be affected the most if civil war breaks out in Afghanistan resulting in an exodus of refugees through its porous borders with these countries.

Turkmenistan is likely to resort to its policy of principled neutrality and maintain cordial relations with Afghanistan irrespective of which Government is in power in Kabul.

Despite having no borders with Afghanistan, Kazakhstan sees itself as a key economic partner for Kabul. It is the only Central Asian country that has an Assistance Programme for the Reconstruction of Afghanistan, which includes modest projects related to water supply, infrastructure development and the delivery of cement and construction commodities. Astana has, for instance, financed the renovation of the Kunduz-Talukan road and the construction of a school and a hospital, spending a total of $2 million. More importantly, as its exports began to take off in 2002, Kazakhstan positioned itself as a major actor in Afghanistan's wheat market. Today, about 20 per cent of Afghan flour imports come from Kazakhstan, and during the years of the Pakistani ban on cereal exports, Kazakhstan even became Afghanistan's main supplier of wheat. Kazakhstan has also offered to train 1,000 Afghan students by investing an amount of $50 million over a period of 5 years; this is yielding positive and encouraging results.

It is likely that if the Central Government in Kabul were to come under severe pressure from Taliban forces from the east and south of the country, dormant organisations like IMU in the Farghana valley will get emboldened, empowered and strengthened to carry out militant activities with greater vigour and energy. This would be immensely detrimental to peace, stability and security of these countries. However, since the regional security landscape is largely undermined by unresolved disputes between Uzbekistan, Kyrgyzstan and Tajikistan, the current efficacy of comprehensive cooperation at the regional level remains uncertain and doubtful. These countries can be expected to seal their boundaries as the date for withdrawal of US and coalition forces approaches.

The Obama Administration is putting it out as though the withdrawal is a great achievement, since it will pull it out of the quagmire that it has been stuck in ever since George Bush declared a "global war on terror." But the reality is not quite so bright. In simple words it can be seen as being close to an abject retreat that can have baleful consequences for others. The departure of the Americans and their allies is a deeply disturbing and anxious moment for the United States, Afghanistan and the neighbouring countries.

Early this year, representatives of India, Russia and China met in Moscow to discuss the emerging scenario in Afghanistan. The discussions were apparently businesslike and devoid of niceties and diplomatese that sometimes mark such parleys. Faced with the rapidly evolving situation, the three regional powers are in active consultation with each other to see what they can do to stabilise the situation. Each of them has interests there, and none of these really clash.

All three countries have an interest in ensuring that Afghanistan is stable and secure, experiences economic growth and reconstruction, and is integrated into the regional economy. India and China are interested in ensuring that a war-ravaged Afghanistan does not once again become a place where militants are able to establish training camps freely. Both have important investments – India's $ 2 billion are spread in development projects to promote Afghan stability, while China's $ 3 billion could contribute to Afghan prosperity. In addition to the investments in hydrocarbons as well as mineral resources in Afghanistan, China is keen that terrorist and Islamic fundamentalist elements are not able to create disturbances in its Xinjiang region and to incite them against the local Han population or the government in Beijing. However whether it would be willing to take any proactive action to protect its interests is a moot point. As for Russia, it is the primary security provider to the Central Asian States and has an interest in preventing the return to a situation of civil war.

It is important that the post-U.S. situation does not degenerate into a battlefield of India-Pakistan rivalry. New Delhi's strategy must be to prevent Islamabad from trying to turn the Afghan clock back to the pre-American, pre-2001 days. In this, it can fruitfully use the dialogue processes it has established with Russia and China and, separately with the U.S. In the recent India-China-Russia talks, the Chinese pointedly avoided projecting Islamabad's case and spoke for their own interests, just as the other interlocutors did.

As for Pakistan, the belief among some key players, notably in the Army, that there can once again be victory in Kabul and the clock can be turned back to pre 2001 days is delusional. Nothing in the ground situation suggests that the writ of the Taliban will run across

Afghanistan again, at least not the Taliban that Pakistan so effectively aided and controlled in the 1990s. Indeed, the most unstable part of the country is likely to be the eastern region bordering Pakistan, whose own border with Afghanistan is the site of an insurgency led by the Haqqani Network and the Tehreek-e-Taliban, Pakistan (TTP). If anything, the TTP could be the principal beneficiary of the withdrawal, since it will find it easier to get sanctuary and arms from the Taliban. Much will of course depend on the policies initiated by the new Government in Pakistan under Nawaz Sharif that will take over the reins of administration in the coming days.

A big problem is that both Islamabad and Taliban are merely hedging their responses to the West and are waiting to see how precipitous the American retreat is, and what happens in the run-up to the Afghan elections of 2014.Though Islamabad says it is supporting the Doha process, there are doubts as to whether or not Pakistan can actually "deliver" the Taliban to the U.S. and its allies. But there can be few doubts about Islamabad's ability to play the spoiler. This is what countries like the US, India, Russia and China need to prevent through coordinated diplomacy.

Another initiative to deal with the situation emerging in Afghanistan emanated from Istanbul in November 2011 in the so-called "Heart of Asia" group. This group is comprised of 14 countries, including all the five Central Asian republics, Russia, China, India, Pakistan, Turkey, Iran, Saudi Arabia, the United Arab Emirates and Afghanistan itself. Concurrently, the United States, Canada, the European Union, the United Nations, Japan and seven European countries enjoy the status of observers. The purpose of the first Istanbul gathering was to pave the way for a sustainable process of reconstruction and reconciliation in Afghanistan through the support of its nation-building efforts in view of US and ISAF's upcoming departure.

In June 2012, a second meeting of the "Heart of Asia" countries was organized in Kabul. The outcome of the meeting was the establishment of a new institutional framework composed of seven working groups covering such issues as trade and economic cooperation, humanitarian assistance, disaster response, joint anti-terrorist and anti-narcotics operations, etc. The conference also highlighted Afghanistan's gradual rapprochement with Central Asia's regional blocs, namely the Shanghai Cooperation Organization (SCO) and the Russian-sponsored Collective Security Treaty Organisation (CSTO). The last SCO summit hosted by China in early June, days before the launch of the "Heart of Asia" follow-up event, had conferred observer status on Afghanistan. In its turn, the CSTO unveiled plans to strengthen cooperation between Member States, basing them on highly negative forecasts with regard to the post-2014 situation in Afghanistan and its impact on regional security in post-Soviet Central Asia. The next meeting of countries under the Istanbul Initiative has taken place in Almaty, Kazakhstan in April, 2013, and can be expected to provide a significant impetus to the process.

With the date of NATO's departure drawing closer, the Central Asian Republics (CARs) have become more active in engaging their external partners, both bilaterally and multilaterally, in coordinated talks for ensuring further stabilization of Afghanistan's domestic situation. Moreover, the scant progress achieved on the Afghan issue during and after Kazakhstan's chairmanship of the OSCE in 2010 has shown the intractable nature of this problem. The future of Central Asia's stability after the West's withdrawal from Afghanistan could be determined by the positions of India, Russia and China and collaboration amongst them to encouraging results deal with the emerging situation.

The SCO, which has been on the sidelines until now is gearing up to assume a bigger role in Afghanistan. Afghanistan has been on the Agenda of the Annual SCO summits for the past several years. Before Afghanistan was admitted as an Observer to SCO in June, 2012, President Karzai used to participate as a Special Invitee in these deliberations. The SCO Peace Mission Joint Military Exercises which started in 2003 on a modest and limited scale have expanded in scope and intensity in recent years. This could partly be in response to the emerging situation in Afghanistan. The SCO countries currently seem to lack the will or inclination to engage substantively in security operations in Afghanistan.

There are encouraging indications that Afghanistan will increasingly integrate with Central Asia in the post-

2014 phase. Afghanistan enjoys the potential to emerge as a transit hub between the Indian subcontinent and Central Asia. Apart from the Turkmenistan-Afghanistan-Pakistan-India (TAPI) gas pipeline, it can earn substantial revenue from overland trade. The 'New Silk Road' strategy propounded in 2011 by USA also seeks to transform Afghanistan into a hub of exchange in trade, energy, business and people-to people contacts between the East and West.

Greater and more active cooperation between the CSTO and NATO can also be envisaged in the post-2014 phase. The Russians and Chinese both realise that although the NATO presence so close to their borders is undesirable, it does provide security to Afghanistan and should be continued to the maximum extent in future. China has benefitted enormously from the security provided by international forces for its investments in Afghanistan. Russia understands the adverse effects of a radical dispensation in Kabul and would support future efforts to provide security to a liberal and democratic government in Afghanistan. Thus, cooperation among rivals is a possibility.

Russia has no intentions of getting involved again in Afghanistan. Russia has not forgotten its humiliation in Afghanistan during its intervention of 1979-89. However, it would be inclined to play a positive role overall. Approximately 40 per cent of logistics supplies for the ISAF now transit via the Northern Distribution Network through Russia and Central Asia. At present Moscow does not allow the use of this route for lethal equipment. However, it may relent on this requirement and may also allow the use of its air bases in Central Asia, provide refuelling facilities and help in search and rescue.

The rulers of the former Soviet republics neighboring on Afghanistan are apprehensive and nervous. The former Soviet Republics of the Region want Russia to stand beside them and hold their hands at the crucial moment. They also want Russia to be more actively involved in Afghan affairs. That is the last thing Russia wants to do alone on its own. It is in no position to end the drug trade, the insurgency and the corruption, which NATO could not stop. It has no intention of putting its own footprint on the country again.

The present situation in Afghanistan is a stalemate at both strategic and tactical levels. Afghanistan has emerged as a treasure trove of mineral deposits (estimates vary between $1 and 3 trillion), but it is China that has benefited the most so far. For example, China signed a $2.9 billion agreement with Kabul in December 2007 to extract copper from the Aynak deposit, which is estimated to contain 240 million tons of ore.

Iran has followed a wait-and-watch policy since the US-led invasion in 2001. In 1998-99, it had amassed 200,000 troops and Revolutionary Guards on its borders with Afghanistan to prevent drug trafficking and protect its territorial integrity. Even now its troops are in stand-by mode close to Afghanistan's western border to prevent cross-border Taliban influence. Iran may allow the use of the road from Chabahar port to Zaranj to open up a new route for logistic supplies, thereby reducing dependence on the two routes that pass through Pakistan's Quetta and Peshawar.

Pakistan stands accused of having an equivocal stance on the international counter-insurgency campaign and providing a safe haven to the Taliban and al-Qaeda in FATA and Baluchistan. Moreover, the military and security agencies, particularly the ISI, continue to seek 'strategic depth' in Afghanistan, with a view to limiting India's influence in Kabul and ensuring Pakistan has significant leverage in any future peace talks in Afghanistan. The ISI in particular fears talks being held on terms too favourable to Washington and Kabul, and is therefore unlikely to alter its stance.

A hasty withdrawal without viable alternative security arrangements could lead to the return of the Taliban and contribute further to regional instability. Instability in Afghanistan will fuel Islamist fundamentalist terrorism and assist the return of the al Qaeda. Serious potential repercussions of an Afghan meltdown include renewed activity of possible transnational terrorism and exacerbated instability in Central Asia and the nuclear-armed subcontinent as thousands flee and the fragile neighbouring countries are dragged into the vortex of regional politics. Once such consequences start appearing, they will be impossible to roll back.

India›s approach must be informed with the recognition that political support for the occupation of Afghanistan has all but evaporated in the West. Second, India must acknowledge the importance of engaging the Taliban and underline its own readiness to talk to its leaders when they come out of the Pakistan army›s shadow. At the same time, India must remind its Western interlocutors that appeasing the Taliban will break the fragile internal balance between the Pashtuns and the non-Pashtun minorities. Third, India must signal its recognition that any durable political settlement in Afghanistan would require addressing Pakistan›s legitimate interests, but will not accept their definition by Rawalpindi. Fourth, India should welcome the prospects of a genuine reconciliation between Pakistan and Afghanistan, so critical for the stability of its north-western frontiers.

Afghanistan has recorded some impressive achievements which are highly praiseworthy. Girls are going to school, the security situation in northern and western parts has improved and some developmental activity has taken place, thanks to the aid and assistance from the international community. The Afghan security forces have also been able to put up a tough fight against the Taliban in several areas. If given consistent and sustained support by the international community, they may be able to get the better of the Taliban. However the Afghan government suffers from several institutional weaknesses that need to be addressed. That is where India can come in.

India, by adopting a low-key role in the last few years, has set itself apart as a country which is genuinely interested in reconstruction and development. India's small-budget interventions in Pashtun areas have been well-received by the population in areas infested by the militants. This has compelled even the Taliban to grudgingly acknowledge India's constructive role. The Strategic Partnership Agreement between the two countries allows India to strengthen linkages in the security sector too. The common Afghan, irrespective of ethnicity, is keen that India continues to play a bigger role in stabilising Afghanistan. In contrast, Pakistan has lost credibility among the Afghans who consider it as a country which does not have anything positive to offer.

India will need to ensure that its role is not misconstrued as interference. India has historically had warm and friendly ties with Afghanistan and wishes to see a stable government installed in Kabul. It has funded several Afghan reconstruction and development projects totaling $2 billion so far. These include construction of the 218 km-long Zaranj-Delaram road linking the Iranian border with the Garland Highway, electric power lines including one from the CARs to Kabul, hydroelectric power projects, school buildings, primary health centres and the new building for the Afghan Parliament. India is also training Afghan administrators, teachers and officer cadets.

India can increase the number of developmental projects in Afghanistan, offer larger number of scholarships to Afghan students, relax visa procedures for Afghan businessmen, students and patients seeking medical attention in India, and encourage the private sector to invest in areas related to education, IT, healthcare systems, aviation, mining, media and communication. Afghanistan is in urgent need of measures to boost its revenue generating capacity. India can contribute in the field of revitalizing agriculture, building infrastructure (railroads, highways, processing plants, etc.), which could spur long-term economic growth and create jobs. It can also help in building of institutions that will stabilise the process of democratization.

The India-Afghanistan relationship must go beyond aid and build a comprehensive security and economic relationship. It would also be worthwhile to contemplate a Free Trade Agreement (FTA). The recent Delhi Investment Summit on Afghanistan is a good beginning that must be sustained.

India should also strive to be part of multilateral efforts, particularly those launched by the SCO, CSTO, NATO etc.

India must not allow its Afghan policy to become hostage to its tense and difficult relations with Pakistan. India's policy in Afghanistan must stay Afghan-centric and not be excessively influenced by Pakistani efforts to gain strategic depth.

Session II

Second Paper

Dr Skandarsek Ayazbekov

Afghanistan And Central Asia: Search For New Civilised Paradigm of Regional Cooperation

Afghanistan, located at the junction of a number of world and local civilizations such as Indian, Chinese, Iranian, Middle Asian and Arab Islamic, it has a special geostrategic meaning in its centuries-old history. Thus, the country has constantly been affected being at the intersection of various geopolitical interests of great powers as well as the Middle East, South and Central Asia. Nowadays geopolitical factor has focused attention of international experts in search of new forms of regional cooperation. Due to the current social-economic and domestic situation in Afghanistan, it could affect the safety and security both at regional and international levels.

It is known that Afghanistan has been facing crisis for more than 30 years. She has withstood invasions of foreign troops as well as bloody civil war. There are terrorist groups, connected with Al Qaeda, Taliban and other Islamic groups, operating in the country. Economic and domestic political situation, despite foreign assistance and central government efforts, is in a very difficult situation. Afghanistan has once again been placed at the epicentre of regional and world politics. There is a range of challenges and threats that exist due to troop withdrawal of the US and NATO Forces by end of 2014.

According to leading international analysts these risks are driven by two interconnected factors:-

(a) Difficult domestic, political, economic and ethno-religious situation.

(b) Various scenarios of geopolitical developments in the region.

We are talking about a totally new approach to the actual geopolitical contradictions, which from our point of view have military, economic and political connotations. As all these factors represent external manifestations of national and geopolitical interests having differences between western and eastern civilizations. Accelerated modernization or forced imposition of other traditions and values inevitably raise interreligious, interethnic, intercultural disputes. Moreover, if it is multiplied by geopolitical, military, strategic and economic interests, the complex scenario can lead to war.

In Afghanistan ethno cultural mosaic of Pashtuns and minorities – Hazaras, Uzbeks, Tajiks and others represents contradictions. There is a similar difficulty between Sunnis and Shiites, and more than 40 other groups in Islam. Not accidently, ethnic groups and Islamic groups have frequent clashes leading to frequent fueds.

Escalating problem of Afghanistan is far beyond the scope of regional security and access to the epicentre of international politics is largely due to the presence since 2001 of the Western coalition, which has become a key factor in different scenarios both in Afghanistan and at regional and global levels, including interaction of different civilizations of the East and the West.

The tasks set by the United States and other Western countries were to: eliminate Bin Laden, overthrow the Taliban regime and bring a framework of democratic setup in Afghanistan. These have mostly been achieved. What remains is to give full control of the Afghan government, the military and law enforcement agencies under the authority of the central government. However, as we all know, the real situation and the immediate prospects are not so bright.

In addition to the geopolitical interests of the leading world and regional powers represented by the United States, China, Russia, India, Iran, and the EU and the former Soviet states of Central Asia, there are conflicts between different ethnic groups and their representative political forces and clans among regional elite, the military and the clergy in Afghanistan.

It should also be noted that in addition to the uncertainty of various geopolitical scenarios, the Afghan problem is directly related to two threats, which have, not only regional but also global character. Firstly terrorism and secondly drugs. These are likely to worsen after the withdrawal of coalition troops in 2014. Focused attention and neutralization of these two threats anticipate an integrated approach, involving many states.

However, we would like to emphasize that the presence of above listed threats and challenges; the Afghan problem should not be diabolized and exaggerated. Neighbouring countries such as India, China, Iran, Russia, Kazakhstan and other Eurasian countries are strong enough to provide effective resistance to the challenges. At the regional level, there are multilateral security organizations (NATO, CSTO, SCO, CICA). A joint consultation has been conducted, not only within the region but also at the international security level with strategic allies and partners.

The search of new formulae of safety is not only at the multilateral level but also at bilateral level. In particular, Kazakhstan is actively involved in the rehabilitation of Afghanistan's economy. It conducts training for experts in the Afghan economy, industry, finance, transportation, and education, and promotes the involvement of Afghanistan in the integration process.

Pragmatic position of Kazakhstan is connected to the fact that the future development of Afghanistan is directly linked to the need for comprehensive approach to development of regional security in Central Asia and South Asia. Divergence of views on the future of Afghanistan and Central Asia could become a major obstacle to regional cooperation after withdrawal of NATO troops in 2014.

This dilemma is related not only to the objective and contradiction of interests, but also to misunderstanding, different values and beliefs about the world. And in our view, requires not only military and political consultations, multilateral economic assistance, but also the active promotion of the main idea of our time - convergence and interaction of civilizations in East and the West. Moreover, today, in the era of globalization, there can be no security without a country developing security at the national, regional and global levels. The situation in Afghanistan has global connotations and solution needs to be found at that level.

References

1. Huntington S. The Collision of Civilizations? // Polis. - 1994. - № 1. - S. 33-48.

2. Havel V. The New Measure of Man // New York Times. -1994. - 8 July. - P. A27.

3. Delors J. Questions Concerning European Security. - International Institute for Strategic Studies, Brussels. - 1993. - 10 September. - P. 2.

Session II

Third Paper

Ambassador Sapar Berdiniyazov

Turkmenistan's Policy in The Region And The Afghan Issue

Today under the great leadership of the President of Turkmenistan H.E. Gurbanguly Berdimuhamedov, Turkmenistan is engaged actively in international relations and participates in global economic processes, guided by the fundamentals of Turkmen Foreign Policy based on neutrality, openness, peace and security. Thus Turkmenistan has established diplomatic relations with 131 countries and trade and economic relations with more than 103 countries. Turkmenistan is already member of 40 International Organizations like the Commonwealth of Independent States (CIS), the Organisation of Islamic Countries (OIC) Economic Cooperation Organisation (ECO) and Non Aligned Movement (NAM) .

This year, it is the Twenty Second anniversary of Independence of our Nation. Though we got independence in 1991 but we are the custodians of one of the most ancient civilizations of the world, as the History of Turkmen people goes back to 5000 B.C.: to the period of Oguz Khan, when the foundation of the first Turkmen state was laid.

The reforms of H.E. Gurbanguly Berdimuhamedov are wide ranging in scale and based on large international co-operation. In his state policy, he underlined the idea that "Policy should serve economy". Today Turkmenistan engages actively in international relations and particularly in global economic processes. The Neutrality of Turkmenistan has been wholeheartedly supported by the people. On the memorable day of December 12, 1995, at the 50th anniversary session of the United Nations General Assembly a special resolution was unanimously adopted by all the 185 state-members of the United Nations (UN) which confirmed the status of the permanent neutrality of Turkmenistan. This event, serves as an illustration of high appreciation of world community of the policy pursued by Independent Turkmenistan based on principals of peacefulness, humanism and openness.

Status of permanent neutrality is not only a recognized phenomenon in the system of international relations, but also a mechanism that ensures the geopolitical interests of the country. This is very important, bearing in mind Turkmenistan's geopolitical location, general situation in the region and the Asian continent as whole.

The fundamentals of Turkmen Foreign Policy are openness, freedom and a readiness to absorb any idea for the betterment of life, peace and security, that can be achieved with concerted efforts of the International community through a UN mechanism. The foreign policy doctrine encompasses the strengthening of the country's independence, preservation and promotion of peace, dynamic development of the national economy and implementation of market reforms. On the basis of these principals Turkmenistan engages actively in international relations and global economic processes. Foreign policy of Turkmenistan based on positive neutral status and maintaining, strengthening and developing the high level of political, economic and cultural relations between fraternal and friendly countries. In 2007 the Opening of the Regional Center of Preventing Diplomacy of the UN in Ashgabat is a historic event for the world community. The fact that Ashgabat was chosen as headquarter of the organization of the UN has a deep meaning. In the 21st century Turkmenistan, which constantly follows the status of permanent Neutrality seeks to bring about political stability with economic cooperation for the benefits of peoples and countries in the region. Turkmenistan follows the way of solving the most important problems with new methods, maintaining the stability not only in the region but also in the whole world, and wide international co-operation for the sake of global security.

Today the world community is interested in peace and stability in Afghanistan, which is very significant not only for its close neighbours but for the whole world. In this context I would like to note that Turkmenistan stands firmly on the position of peaceful and political settlement of Afghan situation. Our practical proposals regarding Afghanistan are based on necessity to use political resources of the countries and international organizations in order to work out new ways oriented to resolve all the issues in Afghanistan only through diplomatic means and methods.

A coordinated role must be played by United Nations (UN) and its designated agencies. Today UN already has got effective tools in relations to Afghan problem. By using the potentials of such agencies as United Nations Afghan Mission for Afghanistan (UNAMA), UN Regional Center for Preventing Diplomacy in Central Asia and the United Nations Development Programme (UND) it is quite real to promptly achieve new political level or resolving problems in Afghanistan. At the same time we all understand that it is up to Afghans themselves to find a key solution. And the world Community should assist the process of inter-afghan settlement.

As it's well known, Turkmenistan strives to do its best for establishing peace and harmony, for rebuilding of economy and social infrastructure of Afghanistan. The President of Turkmenistan moved forward important issues of international policy. These initiatives include the assistance to Afghanistan and development of its regional integration. Turkmenistan projects permanent peace, stability and security in Afghanistan, all problems of the country should be solved through peaceful talks with the neighbouring countries based on international laws, new political and economical tools should be created for long-term development of Afghanistan. In this regard Turkmenistan considers that UN, especially UNAMA and UN Preventive Diplomacy Center in Central Asia can play an important role in establishing peace and stability in that country.

In accordance with its intentions in September 2010 at the 65th UN session, the President of Turkmenistan Mr. Gurbanguly Berdimuhamedov suggested to organise a high-level international meeting under the aegis of UN to discuss the measures for creating trust and consensus, and developing the government structure in Afghanistan. Turkmenistan's initiatives were also discussed at the Istanbul summit (November 2011) and at the Bonn conferences on Afghanistan (December 2011). These initiatives were supported at the Preparatory Meetings for Kabul talks at the Ministerial level. At the 65th session of UN President of Turkmenistan G. Berdimuhamedov offered suggestions for the settlement of the situation in Afghanistan They are:

Firstly; Turkmenistan understands and supports efforts for the management of the situation in Afghanistan, creation of an atmosphere for national consensus and reconciliation in the country. It corresponds with Turkmenistan's vision of development of the inter-afghan processes, and Afghan partners will get all the necessary assistance rendered by the world community.

Secondly; Being guided by desire to promote economic development of this country in business and in the state building process in accordance of the results of the London and Kabul meetings, we offer the help in preparing in Turkmenistan home nursing and other programmes of the UN on Afghan management structures in various branches.

Thirdly; Turkmenistan considers the major problem in rendering assistance to Afghanistan as the lack of a transport infrastructure.

Our Country offers the civil-engineering design of the railway from Turkmenistan to Afghanistan with prospect of its further continuation in the Afghan territory with participation of the international organizations, countries-donors and international financial institutions. We would welcome cooperation with the world community.

Fourthly: Turkmenistan considers the urgent need to make intense and active efforts directed on building of a gas pipeline Turkmenistan-Afghanistan-Pakistan-India (TAPI). The Trans-afghan gas pipeline can make essential impact on development of economy of Afghanistan; help to solve large social problems, including employment, to promote and attract of investments, which would have a positive impact on political conditions in the country.

Fifthly: Turkmenistan is ready to consider and increase in deliveries of the electric energy to Afghanistan, and also expansions of the energy infrastructure which in the long run would add to the capacities in the

Afghan territory. Turkmenistan invites the international community in the name of the United Nations to discussion of this offer.

Turkmenistan pays great attention to the establishment of trade and economic ties with the countries of the region. In this regard TAPI gas pipeline project should be mentioned. Joint work on the pipeline has commenced. The construction of the pipeline will be beneficial for the development of economy of the region; especially it holds great importance for Afghan people and the economy of the country. After the implementation of this project Afghanistan will earn annually more than USD 300 million as a transit country. At the same time it is expected that nearly 12 thousand job places will be created.

The most important component in comprehensive development of Afghanistan is strengthening international efforts aimed at reconstruction of economic and social infrastructure, and active involvement in regional and global trade and economic processes, as well as implementation of major energy and transport projects.

In Turkmenistan's perception the creation of transport infrastructure.is crucial and it accords high priority to it. In this connection in May 2011 on the sidelines of the Official visit of the President of Afghanistan to Turkmenistan, "Atamyrat - Imamnazar (Turkmenistan) – Akina – Andhoy (Afghanistan) agreement for a railway project was signed.

Increasing dynamics of Turkmen – Afghan cooperation is evident in the sphere of trade-economic cooperation between two countries, as well as in the projects related to transport and energy infrastructure. Turkmenistan supplies electricity to Afghanistan on preferential price. Liquefied gas, diesel and gasoline and other items are also supplied.

One of the main points of trade-economic cooperation between two countries is power supply. Turkmenistan annually provides 362 million KWT worth USD 7.2 million. In future Turkmenistan intends to increase power supply to Afghanistan.

In February 2011, President of Turkmenistan G. Berdimuhamedov signed a Decree about construction of Mary –

Lebap – Afghanistan, 500 KWT high voltage power transmission line and construction of small power transmission units. After the completion of the construction, power supply to Afghanistan will increase up to 1.5 billion KW annually. Already 40 per cent of construction has been completed and the project should be fully completed by the end of 2013. In order to connect power lines of both countries Afghanistan with the assistance of international organizations and financial institutions should build new power transmission units in its territory. The implementation of the above mentioned projects will give an opportunity to increase power supply to Afghanistan itself and sell Turkmen power to other countries through its territory.

Turkmenistan is a close neighbour of Afghanistan, and we are linked with commonality of two nations' culture, traditions and customs, that have a century long history. Friendly and brotherly relations between our countries are getting enriched day by day, and becoming solid and firm foundation for their further development and strengthening on the long-term basis. Turkmenistan attaches immense importance to the development of bilateral ties with Afghanistan and by all means will facilitate their further deepening in all spheres of activity.

Turkmenistan and Afghanistan actively cooperate with each other within the frameworks of international organizations, particularly within the UN system. On the level of the United Nations Organization close partnership is based on mutual interest, international peace and stability, security, and development. The Joint Commission for Trade – Economic is very important component of bilateral relations and is facilitating the process of exploration of fruitful forms of partnership and the establishment of mutually beneficial cooperation on a long-term basis.

One of Turkmenistan's cardinal foreign policy principle is to develop neighbourhood relations. Turkmenistan continues supporting Afghanistan through reasonable assistance in other important fields such as healthcare and education. Turkmenistan provides free-of-charge medical services to the population of border regions. In 2012 on the territory of Afghanistan Turkmen side has constructed school and health centre.

Promoting and fostering education in Afghanistan is also very important, especially in terms of training Afghan nationals for different sectors of economy and governance.

During last several years Turkmenistan assisted in training highly qualified Afghan personnel. An agreement on education also was signed. According to this agreement currently 76 young people study at the universities, institutes and technical schools of Turkmenistan. It should be noted that currently a new system of international cooperation is active in order to create full-scale dialogue on Afghanistan, with the main goal of reconstruction of Afghanistan. High level meetings held in 2011 in Istanbul and Bonn, and recently – in May 2012 in Chicago are examples of an integrated approach to ensure peace and stability in Afghanistan.

In this context, the stress on regional cooperation, within the framework of Istanbul process, in Turkmenistan opinion, is an effective mechanism that can radically alter the situation in Afghanistan and beyond.

It should be noted that Turkmenistan has always been supportive of resolutions of the situation in Afghanistan that have emphasized only peaceful and political means. This way it can bring long-lasting peace in our neighbourhood. In order to implement this principle, President Gurbanguly Berdimuhamedov put forward the initiative of UN sponsored peace talks on Afghanistan with the participation of all interested parties, and expressed readiness to host such peace talks.

Political settlement cannot be complete and lasting without real economic development; effective fight against terrorism and drug trafficking is impossible without solution of social problems and improvement of education and culture. Turkmenistan confirms its participation in areas such as regional infrastructure, education, activities of chambers of commerce and industries. Turkmenistan is ready to coordinate implementation of "Confidence-Building Measures". As you know, number of countries, regional and international organizations took a decision to participate in the implementation of CBMs. Altogether there were 6 CBMs.

Turkmenistan participated in three of them: **"Regional Infrastructure the implementation"** CBM; with the participation from Afghanistan, India, Iran, Kazakhstan, Russian Federation and Turkey, CBM's in Trade and Chambers of Commerce together with Afghanistan, India, Iran, Russian Federation, Tajikistan and Turkey. In this sphere India is leading; CBM's in education, with the cooperation of Turkmenistan and participants from Afghanistan, India, Iran, Kazakhstan, Pakistan, Russian Federation and Tajikistan, in this sphere of education Iran is leading.

Turkmenistan recognizes the important role of the regional organizations covering different combinations of the "Heart of Asia" countries. In particular, we highlight the role of Organization for Islamic Cooperation (OIC), the Shanghai Cooperation Organization (SCO), the South Asian Association for Regional Cooperation (SAARC), the Regional Economic Cooperation Conference on Afghanistan (RECCA), the Conference on Interaction and Confidence Building Measures in Asia (CICA), the Economic Cooperation Organization (ECO), the Commonwealth of Independent States (CIS), the Eurasian Economic Union (EEU), the Eurasian Economic Community (EurAsEC), the Organization for Security and Cooperation in Europe (OSCE), the Collective Security Treaty Organization (CSTO), the United Nations Special Programme for the Economies of Central Asia (UNSPECA), and the Central Asia Regional Economic Cooperation (CAREC), in the context of regional cooperation towards enhanced security and economic development in the region.

Our approach in this sphere is based on a clear understanding of priorities and existing opportunities for development of regional infrastructure. Turkmenistan has clear vision and concrete plans of cooperation with Afghanistan and other neighbours, and has experience of already implemented major infrastructure projects. In this regard, we believe that implementation of large-scale projects, initiated by the President of Turkmenistan, are of great importance. Among them; Turkmenistan – Afghanistan – Pakistan – India gas pipeline project, Turkmenistan – Afghanistan railway project and construction of new infrastructure for significant increase of electricity supply from Turkmenistan in the Afghan direction.

Our today's meeting is a demonstration of our commitment to achieve the goals set and our confidence in achieving concrete results. Unification of our efforts, which are based on goodwill, mutual trust and support of the United Nations and other major and reputable international and regional organizations, is essential for effectiveness of our joint activity for peaceful development of brotherly Afghanistan.

In conclusion, I would like to express my gratitude for excellent organization of this conference and good conditions for its fruitful work. And special thanks goes to all diplomats and experts for their professional work.

Session II

Fourth Paper

Dr (Ms) Zamira Muratalieva

Regional Security of Central Asia: Problems And Prospects

Central Asia is an international political region that has emerged recently (after 1991) and it is still in the process of formation. In view of the quite stable but paradoxically stagnating situation in Central Asia there is a probability of significant geopolitical, political, social and cultural changes in the mid-term perspective. And these changes, in any case, will influence the regional security. Transformation processes are characterized by radical and structural changes with a new type of a social system that is connected with the dismantlement of the old system. Elimination of the old to security elements, as it doesn't answer the new realities and contemporary level of social development can materialize in the mid-term perspective for a number of reasons. Certainly, it is possible to assert that military forces withdrawal from Afghanistan and the coalition intention, to provide military and technical assistance to the Central Asian countries including weapons, will create a new situation in the security sphere.

Eastern Europe countries have found their geopolitical direction and created their security architect after the collapse of the USSR. But that is not the same for the Central Asian countries undergoing transition period that can be defined as a "system punishment". Central Asia can be characterized by the "three no" rule: uncertainty, instability and unpredictability. There is no fully functional regional security architect in Eurasia as is in Europe, that is based on the North Atlantic Treaty Organisation (NATO), The European Union (EU) and The Organisation for Security and Cooperation in Europe (OSCE). Nevertheless there are some factors that can initiate transformation processes and influence the security situation in the future. They are as follows: external geopolitical actor's activity and problems connected with internal political processes. Absence of authoritative succession mechanisms in Kazakhstan, Uzbekistan and Tajikistan and two unconstitutional regime changes in the sovereign history of Kyrgyzstan determine uncertainty in the choice of the following political development vector.

Besides that, the Central Asian region demonstrates its geopolitical imbalance in the aspect of international security: some regional countries take part simultaneously in the NATO programs being members of the Shanghai Cooperation Organization,(SCO) Collective Security Treaty Organization, Organization(CSTO) and in Islamic Conference and Organization of Economic Cooperation. Most of the experts connect their hopes of Eurasia and Central Asia security system with the Shanghai Cooperation Organization and Collective Security Treaty Organization.

For the CSTO the year 2012 was a milestone 10 years since the official appearance of the organization, and 20 years since the signing of the Collective Security Treaty in Tashkent. However, the weight, credibility and prospects of the CSTO in the absence of an elaboration of its concept, its vision its place and role in world security is still doubtful.

Despite the presence of its own military structure, the CSTO as a military and political alliance, unlike, the NATO, has never been involved in the military operations. There are separate activities aimed at specific targets to fight crime, but as a military alliance the CSTO has never participated in the suppression and elimination of the conflict at the national or regional level.

As an important and positive step, it is the evolution of the CSTO, its agreement with the Allies to have the same position concerning a number of foreign policy issues, as it is between the NATO or EU. In 2011, leaders of the CSTO member-states agreed to station military bases of third powers only on the basis of mutual consent of the Allies. As noted by President Nursultan Nazarbaev of Kazakhstan "now, it is necessary to obtain an official approval of all the member-states of the organization to station a military base of a third country on the territory of CSTO states. The proposal was accepted by all the countries. This is a clear sign of the CSTO member-states' commitment to the allied relations"[1]. Lately it has become the only solution for a coordinated policy. However, this arrangement is only a formal declaration taking into account the lack of accountability of the member-states for their decisions and the possibility for them to leave or re-enter the organization.

The conditions for the beginning of the CSTO institutional reforms and strategy design that must not be just a declaration in written form, which cannot be realized is a thing of past. Obviously, it is necessary to make the organization attractive for the member-states in order the number of countries wishing to join it will be more rather than to leave it, taking into account that for the last 20 years 3 states out of 12 have left the structure (Georgia, Azerbaijan, Uzbekistan). In order to do so, first of all, it is necessary to elaborate a strategy and consolidate the conceptual framework that answers the current requirements for the maintenance of security and stability in the member-states. The CSTO member-states' leaders don't have consensus on the objectives, main mission, and most importantly, the vectors of the future development of the organization. And this clouds the CSTO prospects. In this regard, the decision to create an information-analytical structure within the CSTO that will enlarge the strategies and concepts of the organization gives hope, about its future development.

Probably, against the background of Uzbekistan's withdrawal from the CSTO it is time to review the Charter and its procedure. For example, as it is tacitly understood in the NATO "one is not with us is against us". Unfortunately, now it is necessary to note that attempts to build a security system without Uzbekistan are doomed to failure because with its leaving the principle of regional integrity and complexity has been lost.

Another organization concerning security is the Conference on Interaction and Confidence-building Measures in Asia (CICMA) that was officially founded in 1999 with the adoption of the "Declaration of Principles Guiding the CICMA Member-States Relationships" on

---

1 CSTO laid down at stake US Air forces bases / Rosbisneskonsalting. – December 20, 2011

the initiative of President Nazarbaev. This document proclaimed the principles of cooperation, mutual respect, territorial integrity and non-interference in internal affairs, disarmament etc. However, there is just formal declaration of general principles in this organization without any real foundation for their compliance and implementation. Viewed against the background that at the time one of the signatories - Afghanistan – did not control its territory, and India and Pakistan are in a state of permanent conflict. It can be noted that the organization was formed without a realistic assessment of the situation in the region. So, a logical conclusion is that the CICMA has not made any tangible contribution to the security in Asia because there are not any real results in the establishment of trust among the member-states.

Experience of "Shanghai Five" has demonstrated a high and in many ways unique potential of this grouping A special feature of the SCO as a security and stability guarantor along the border areas, is rightly noted by Chinese experts who asserts that no other organization in the region can match it. And the lack of a "cluster" label of SCO could be used to enhance the prestige of the organization. Indeed, in the framework of the SCO a new security system based on partnership rather than alliances seems to be emerging.

However, Beijing is actively using the SCO to their advantage, and thus trying to change the geopolitical balance and the traditional system of internal and external relations of the Central Asian republics. On the other hand, the cooperation between China and Russia within the framework of the SCO is one of the important factors for the strengthening and development of the organization. But Russia and China have different perceptions of the SCO: if the Chinese leadership sees the SCO as an important project of economic integration, Russia sees the main purpose of the organization to ensure the security of the region. In these circumstances, the risk of competition for influence between the two powers is likely to escalate. And for Russia, and China it is extremely important to restrain competition and to develop mutually beneficial cooperation. In this aspect, the SCO is necessary, in our view, to develop jointly with the Member States a long-term strategy for the development of Russian-Chinese partnership in Central Asia. Otherwise, the policy of Russia in the SCO is destined to become ineffective in the region, not able to have any influence on the development of world integration processes. We can agree that the SCO - is not an integrated union and while it is experiencing a fairly prolonged period of searching for its own identity.

A major problem of the SCO is the different levels of economic development of the participating countries. It is the lack of a clear conceptual framework and the containment of the differences among member countries in the understanding of the key geo-economic, geopolitical and even functional tasks in the SCO.

Security cooperation within the SCO is mostly declarative in nature, that is, limited to the adoption of conventions on combating terrorism, separatism and extremism. Unfortunately, we can summarize that the forms of cooperation can be reduced only to the exchange of information, creation of a common database and consensus of member-states on a number of theoretically important issues of the world politics and international relations. Real practical action in the field of military security can be considered such as joint anti-terrorism exercises however, not all the member-states take part.

However, the experience of the SCO in the resolution of common security issues could be of importance to India, Pakistan and Afghanistan through interstate cooperation. SCO experience is useful in the search for a model of the East Asian regional security in the Asia Pacific region. The activities of «six» would be useful to the Pacific Rim countries, and the countries of the Middle East and South Asia as the experience of establishing effective mechanisms for regional security and settlement of disputed border issues. Simultaneously SCO is - an experience of relations between large (Russia, China) and small countries (Central Asia) without prejudice of the latter's interests.

Basing on the current realities the possible vectors of the Central Asian countries security system could be on the following model:

- Improvement of the mechanisms and role of the CSTO and participation in resolving conflicts of various kinds can contribute to the Eurasian integration;

- Increasing role of the SCO with the help of its military component that can lead to a "Chinazation" of the region in the future;

- Absence of any progress in building security architecture. Such an absence could result in Islamization and "chaos" in the region, perhaps even destabilization of Central Asia.

- Western security model is possible against the background of a strengthening role of the NATO, but it seems unlikely;

- Central Asian own way of development in the case of finding its own way of security system building, but at present it is also practically impossible.

The current transformation of Central Asia is taking place in such a way that the region is being simultaneously involved into four different geopolitical projects - the Eurasian Union, the Chinese way, the Western and Islamic model.

In general, it should be noted that despite all the efforts of international organizations to make at least some contribution to the strengthening of security in Central Asia, these are limited to information exchange, joint exercises and mutual assistance in the military-technical equipment, and lack any actual joint actions to address critical security issues.

It is difficult to compare the effectiveness of NATO, with SCO, and the CSTO and CICMA operating almost in isolation and in some ways overlapping each other's activity. These organizations can neither strengthen mutual trust among member-states nor give a single assessment of some of the pressing international issues in order to create a general moral "spirit" and secure uniformity of positions within a single organization.

At present, the region has become the object of a collision of different "geopolitical projects" offered by the key actors of the world politics. Such a geopolitical uncertainty is the result of the Central Asian states "multi-vector" foreign policy with a membership in several international and regional organizations, some of which contradict and overlap each other.

As mentioned above, organizations such as the CICMA, CSTO and SCO overlap each other's activities and therefore it is necessary to delineate these structures in the fields of security and on the stages of participation in solving international problems. Otherwise, if this trend continues to develop there will be a competition between them and unreasonable costs of material and intellectual resources. This situation will ultimately lead to a decrease in the effectiveness of each of these organizations in particular and the whole security architecture of Central Asia.

Session II

Fifth Paper

Mr Aziz Vasikovich Rasulov

Uzbek Perspectives on The Afghan Conundrum

The peaceful settlement of the conflict situation in Afghanistan is one of the most pressing problems of present time. The issue of peace and stability affects not only Afghanistan or its neighbors, but also influences the regional and global security as a whole.

An ongoing conflict for more than 30 years in Afghanistan has destroyed its social and economic infrastructure. This has led to impoverishment of the population and also has led the Afghan people to destitution with no confidence in their own future, which in turn contributes to the continuation and intensification of violence in Afghanistan. The unfortunate state of the people of Afghanistan has been deteriorating with every passing day of the war, complicating the solution of the problem itself.

Despite the considerable efforts undertaken by the international community and the coalition forces to maintain peace and stability in the country, the situation tends to worsen. The announcement of the date withdrawal of coalition forces by the end of 2014 has led to the escalation of armed opposition activities virtually throughout the territory of Afghanistan leading to a new spiral of confrontation in the country.

In these circumstances, the decision adopted in October 2010 in the Lisbon summit of the North Atlantic Treaty Organisation (NATO) on accelerated creation of the Afghan National Security Forces (ANSF) and the gradual transfer of responsibility to these Forces in terms of ensuring security in the country and the step-by-step withdrawal of the International Security Assistance Forces (ISAF) from Afghanistan by the end of 2014 has become today the subject of lively discussions and debates among international experts.

There are various assumptions of possible positive and negative scenarios of the likely situation in Afghanistan, the impact of these developments on neighbouring states and the global balance of power. They all share the view that the coalition efforts did not solve the main problem - the country continues to remain afflicted with terrorism, extremism, drug-trafficking, which closely intertwines with the political instability, internal opposition, economic decline, militarization and geopolitical rivalry among the major and regional powers.

This fact of uncertainty is able to increase the threat of terrorist and extremist activity, leading to heightened tensions and confrontation in the region, which is a permanent source of instability.

In addition, the complicated internal political situation in Afghanistan, and the decline the volume of foreign aid could provide a powerful impetus to illegal activities, especially drug trafficking and transnational crime.

The forthcoming withdrawal of international coalition forces by 2014 has opened up new possibilities and incentives to accelerate the negotiating process between the confronting Afghan parties. However, the fate of reconciliation process is not clear yet. The armed opposition has not demonstrated a serious and sustained interest in peace talks. Hard-line groups within the Taliban and their power base do not feel that they are defeated. Furthermore, non-Pashtun groups have also indicated that they would not support the peace agreement, which does not consider their interests.

The situation is further compounded by the absence of a strong political figure or force in Afghanistan with sufficient authority to consolidate Afghan population and the country as a whole. Undoubtedly, in stabilizing the situation in Afghanistan and its approach to the path of peaceful development, a huge role is also assigned to the international community. The United States, Russia, China and regional powers should and must contribute to this goal. However, the cooperation among the involved countries has often not taken place as the policies they usually pursue are in their own interests. Their approach is to maximize their benefits, undermining the peace settlement in this war-ravaged country.

History of Afghanistan for the last 200 years illustrates that this is not a constructive way, for it could lead to a deadlock and expose the neighboring countries to the threats of extremism and terrorism. In our opinion, the current situation calls for a radical revision of approaches to solving the Afghan crisis and searching possible common ground and compromise solutions, primarily for the benefit of the people of Afghanistan and the region. It becomes more obvious today that there is no military solution of the Afghan crisis. Without addressing issues such as reconstruction of the war-torn economy, communications and social infrastructure of Afghanistan, without engaging Afghans themselves in the process of negotiations and reconstruction positive changes in the situation may be difficult.

It is of vital importance to demonstrate a full respect to the centuries-old traditions, customs and values based on Islam. This can be achieved on this basis, of dialogue and by building up the necessary consensus within Afghanistan. We are confident, that the most important principle of Afghan settlement based on the involvement of all the feuding parties, ethnic, religious and territorial groups and other political forces is absolutely imperative. For without the participation of all political forces, armed conflict will continue. Also it is necessary to coordinate the efforts of all who are interested in the early completion of the war. In the unfolding situation, the most acceptable way to tackle the Afghan problem is to establish the Contact Group under auspices of the United Nations with participation of the countries neighbouring on Afghanistan, as well as the United States, the North Atlantic Treaty Organisation (NATO) and Russia.

The major goal of the Contact Group would be to achieve a compromise and accord between confronting forces, and form on this basis a coalition government which might represent the core ethnic, national and religious groups of Afghanistan involved in the military and political standoff. The guarantees to be provided by the international community are of crucial significance and will have an impact on the negotiating process. They are the following: -

- The territorial integrity, independence and sovereignty of Afghanistan, as well as providing for a peaceful and stable country free of terrorism and drug crimes;

- Full respect towards the centuries-long traditions, customs and values of Islam adhered by the people of country;

- The necessary assistance in reconstructing the devastated economy, implementation of the social and infrastructure projects, as well as tackling unemployment and initiating measures to address poverty and misery.

The Republic of Uzbekistan has always led and shall always pursue a good neighborly and friendly policy towards neighboring Afghanistan. Given the background of rich historical ties and experience, Uzbekistan builds tits relations with Afghanistan on bilateral basis taking into consideration the national interests of both countries and respecting the choice to be made by the Afghan people in terms of the future of their country.

At the same time, we believe that it is important for Uzbekistan not to get involved in the internal Afghan conflict or support any of the various Afghan factions.

Uzbekistan, as a close neighbor of Afghanistan, supports Afghan initiatives by participating in the implementation of concrete projects on peace-building, reconstruction of the economy of the country destroyed by years of war.

The tens of motorway bridges and automobile roads have been built on the territory of Afghanistan. At the moment, Kabul is provided power from transmission lines from the electricity power line "Khairaton – Puli-Humri – Kabul". Afghanistan has joined Uzbekistan's fiber-optical communication line.

Since 2011 the railroad route "Khairaton – Mazari-Shareef", built by the Uzbek specialists, has been functioning which is of special significance for the future of this region. The continuation of construction of the rail link section from "Mazari-Shareef – Shibergan" shall pave the way for implementing the Trans-Afghan transport corridor project which will ensure the shortest route for the transit of goods from Central Asia to seaport.

In conclusion, I would like to emphasize, that Uzbekistan is aware that peace and stability in Afghanistan is crucial to regional and global security. Such a prospect can open huge opportunities for solving critical problems of sustainable social and economic development of all nations and peoples living in Central Asia.

Session- II : Discussion

Afghan Conundrum And Regional Approach

Question - What is the collective response of CARs towards radical Islam and Taliban? Is there any help envisaged from Pakistan?

Response - The Uzbek participant Aziz Rasulov said that this issue should be addressed on a bilateral basis . He however agreed that the people of all the CARs have to be alive to this danger.

Ambassador Sajjanhar said that the CARs should do the following:

- Border Management ; they should close their borders.

- CSTO and the Russians who are the security providers have to take on some role.

- CARs have to work together on intelligence sharing.

- If the CARs feel that it is a common challenge , they should collaborate with each other and manage their borders.

Ayazbekov of Kazakhstan said that the key problem lies in Pakistan and that its participation was necessary in talks of Afghanistan. However, Ambassador Sapar Berdiniyazov differed and said that the key to problem lies with the Al Qaeda and not Pakistan. He mentioned that the collective will of CARs was missing and there is no mechanism within CARs to deal with organisations like the Al Qaeda and Taliban. He also referred to the internal problems in some Central Asian countries which made it difficult to pay attention to external issues. He cautioned that, if the region did not have a coordinated effort against hostile groups, it would be difficult to manage them at a later stage.

Question - What influence does Pakistan's establishment have on the Taliban? Are there any indications of it being controlled by

Pakistan?

Response - Ambassador Sapar Berdiniyazov of Turkmenistan clarified that the Pakistani Army had contacts with Taliban through Tahrik-e-Taliban Pakistan, but whether it had any control over Taliban could not be said with certainty.

Question - What is the assessment of CARs on the Northern Alliance? Does it have linkages with the Northern Alliance?

Response – Ambassador Berdiniyazov clarified the stand of his country and said that Turkmenistan believed in neutrality in view of the weak border with Afghanistan and their desire to keep the border peaceful. He said, for this reason alone, his country interacted with both the Taliban and the Northern Alliance. He also mentioned that terrorism was not the responsibility of CARs alone; all had to fight it collectively.

Uzbek participant said they never had any relations with either of the two – Taliban and Northern Alliance. He said Uzbeks always talked to the government of Afghanistan.

Question - On withdrawal of US/NATO forces in post 2014, do you see a role for Iran being an important member, in solving the Afghan problem?

Response - The delegate from Kyrgyzstan said .that Iran has a role to play in post 2014 Afghanistan because of the following:

- Iran's close ties with the Tajik population.

- The possibility of Iran joining the SCO as a Member.

- Iran's involvement in helping to find a solution to the Afghan imbroglio.

Question - Do you visualize Taliban continuing to operate after 2014 with the changes introduced in the polity by the Karzai government?

Response - Ambassador Berdiniyazov said that the US led forces have contributed to the weakening of the region and the Central Asian countries relationship with Afghanistan. He did not see much hope with regard to the Taliban accepting any changes made by the outsiders.

Question - What are the prospects of stability in Afghanistan? Has anything changed in last three decades and will Afghan war-lords respect central authority after 2014?

Response - Ambassador Ashok Sajjanhar said that nothing much had changed in Afghanistan. He foresaw powerful war-lords taking control of their area of influence as they are strong in their own regions. Ayazbekov, the Kazakh participant mentioned that there were some Islamist groups operating in Afghanistan who are from a Middle East country. Hence these groups will continue to defy the central authority whoever comes to power after 2014.

Session III

Chairperson's Opening Remarks

Ambassador Phunchuk Stobdan (Retd)

We have a very interesting topic in this session "Economic Engagement Reconnecting Central Asia with India. This is something which is extremely important and we are late in this aspect; connecting ourselves with Central Asia. Nonetheless efforts are on at various levels and to speak on this theme we have four very powerful speakers; Professor Nirmala Joshi, Mr Yuriy Makubayev, from Kazakhstan, Ambassador of Turkmenistan in India Mr Parakhat Durdyev and Mr Evgeny Kablukov of Kyrgyzstan Embassy in India. I think we will be able to have twenty to twenty five minutes for each speaker for presentation. We will have two presentations now and three after the tea break in continuation. May I now invite Prof Nirmala Joshi to make her presentation.

Session III

First Paper

Professor Nirmala Joshi

Enhancing India's Economic Engagement With The Central Asian Republics

In Indian Strategic thinking the Central Asian Republics (CARs) are part of its extended neighbourhood. At stake are India's vital security and economic interests. With India's increasing involvement with Afghanistan, these interests have grown manifold times. In Indian perception CARs and Afghanistan belong to same geopolitical space. Since their inception as independent sovereign entities, India's concern has been that the Central Asian region should not be destabilized by forces of extremism and terrorism that had arisen in neighbouring Afghanistan. A secular, modern and a democratic polity is in India's interest. Secondly, in order to keep pace with its growing international profile as an economic power the need for a regular supply of energy is evident and the Central Asian energy wealth provided a significant alternative to India's quest for this vital resource. A complicating factor; however is that CARs are landlocked.

After they gained independence in 1991, the CARs have been caught in the vortex of international politics because of their geographical location in the centre of Eurasia and their wealth of natural resources especially energy resources; oil, natural gas, hydrocarbons and hydel power. With energy security occupying the centre stage of international politics, the post-Soviet space witnessed a competition among major and regional powers to secure, if not, control the resources of Central Asia.

Intertwined with the competition was geopolitics; Halford Mackinder's ideas were reinvented and Eurasia acquired a new relevance in the post-cold war world order. After the collapse of socialism and break-up of the Soviet Union, Russia expected that it would be accepted as a natural partner by the West. But it soon realized that the United States of America and its European allies were not ready to accept it as an equal partner. The West wanted Russia to remain a junior partner; an appendage supplying raw materials. The cold war mind set had not disappeared. Russia was viewed initially as an unstable power with huge ambitions, and later as having the potential to emerge a regional player in Asia. India and China were projected as emerging Asian powers, and Indonesia, Vietnam and other countries of Southeast Asia as fast developing powers. All the emerging players needed energy for their development. In their industrial developmental plans securing uninterrupted supply of energy was crucial. The energy wealth of CARs drew world attention and acquiring this vital resource became a high priority in the foreign policies of the competing powers. Their approach has been exclusive and not inclusive so far. Since the CARs are landlocked building export pipeline infrastructure came as a handy tool in the hands of the competitors. Simultaneously, planning and charting transport routes connecting the region primarily with their own became another tool in the hands of the competing powers. The US and the European Union (E U) on the one hand and China on the other hand are trying to create interdependencies in Central Asia through export pipeline infrastructure and transport routes networks, so as to expand their respective areas of influence. Russia has been since trying to regain its influence in CARs and is still a power to reckon with in Central Asia. As of now major and regional powers have established their strong foot prints in the CARs particularly in the energy sector. The Baku-Tbilisis-Ceyhan (BTC) pipeline carries oil from Azerbaijan bypassing Russia to Turkey, while China has constructed two energy pipelines carrying Kazkh oil and the second one for natural gas from Turkmenistan. Similarly, the US has initiated the concept of 'Greater Central Asia' aimed at connecting Central Asia with South Asia the New Silk Road Strategy is a continuation of the first one. China has launched its Silk Road Initiative to connect with the Caspian Sea region via Central Asia. This competition is likely to get intense once the coalition forces withdraw from Afghanistan. These interests for the present have not reached an inimical stage.

Indian policy towards CARS in the early years of independence was largely reactive and began to gather momentum only by the turn of the century. There was a shift in India's Strategic outlook. It wanted to play a role beyond South Asia. Among the factors that contributed to India's rising international profile were; its emergence as a manufacturing hub, its knowledge based industries and perceived as a rising Asian power. Viewed against this background India was keen to establish a firmer presence in CARs. Although the Taliban has been defeated, the continuing resilience of forces of extremism and terrorism and the existence of terrorist Infrastructure has added to India's concern for the stability and security of CARs. Indian concerns are that an 'Integrated Strategic Region 'oriented towards religion should not arise in its extended neighbourhood. In a way it is an ideological struggle between secular and non-secular forces. Indian interests are in seeing that the modern, secular polities in the CARs are able to confront the challenge of extremism and terrorism. In this regard India and the CARs' interests are congruent.

Today the regional security scenario is entering a critical phase. It can be said with reasonable certainty that a period of uncertainty awaits the region. It is uncertain at present the shape of future Afghan government and the strength of the Taliban In this context the CARs are vulnerable in view of the region's geographical proximity to Afghanistan. Periodic reports suggest that militants often take shelter in Gorno Badkhshan Tajikistan eastern province.

Viewed against this perspective, India would like to increase its footprints in Central Asia. Apart from its rich legacy of historical links and cultural contacts, and its perception as a friendly power by the CARs, one of the tools available to India is to deepen and expand its economic engagement with these countries. The process of transforming their societies is not yet over. This entails hardship and difficulties for the people. As a consequence some are an easy to extremists who lure them into their nefarious activities with monetary incentives. It is essential that initiatives for economic development and reforms are speeded up which to an extent could address some of the grievances. Indian experience in economic reforms could be useful. Possibly Indian experience in its economic reform process could be useful.

Today India's ability to interact with CARS is recognized. At the same time its quest for accessing Central Asian energy has acquired urgency. On the other hand the CARs are responsive to enhance their interaction with India, as their interests are in congruence with their multivector foreign policy objective "No single Power will dominate Central Asia" Besides, the CARs would like to diversify their economies and move away from raw materials exporting countries. Given their intellectual resources they have reached a stage today where they can absorb advanced Indian technology and need support to develop their small and medium industries. Moreover the people of this region are well aware of Indian products and culture and that could prove to be an added advantage. Besides the following observation by former Uzbek Ambassador to India Ibrokhim Mavlanov is pertinent. In his perception "India's economic growth shows that India is not only a reliable business partner, but one of the most experienced countries in the Asian region that can, with its economic potential promote active development in the Central Asian region".

Economic Engagement

In the numerous high level diplomatic exchanges between India and the CARs the economic content in the Joint Statements or Strategic Partnership Agreements is prominent feature. Since India is not a Member of the various regional initiatives, its interaction is at the bilateral level. In this context, mention must be made of the Asian Development Bank's (ADB) Programme the Central Asian Regional Economic Cooperation (CAREC). CAREC Programme focuses on trade, energy and transport in Central Asia. A couple of years ago Pakistan was made a Member, but not India. India's Membership of CAREC should be explored with the ADB. Mention must be made that India is a growing market and a rising economic power, the CARs stand to benefit by enhancing their engagement with India.

Among the areas of cooperation agriculture holds immense promise as it is the mainstay of the economies of CARs. Hence a potential area of cooperation is in the field of agriculture. In all the Central Asian countries cotton is the chief crop and a major source of revenue for them. Exports of cotton have suffered primarily because the CARs are landlocked and also because the financial and economic crisis of 2008 adversely affected exports. Moreover, cotton cultivation requires plenty of water. The two perennial rivers; the AmuDarya and Syrdarya are shrinking and today water is a highly contentious issue among the countries. What is required is to introduce innovative technologies to conserve water such as drip irrigation and water management schemes. Another area of cooperation is remote sensing of the region. Such an exercise could suggest what are alternatives available to CARs in agriculture. India has set up a Joint Working Group in the sphere of textiles with Uzbekistan, whereby textile machinery can be imported from India and engineers trained in India.

A related area for cooperation is in the sphere of light industries such as food processing and packaging. All the countries grow plenty of fruits and have large quantities of dry fruits. At times these products are wasted due to lack of facilities. These products, if well packaged, can be exported. Another potential area for cooperation is assisting in setting up dairy farming and poultries. It is also important to build roads connecting villages with towns, training scientists in agricultural research. India's ITEC programme is useful in this respect. Indian investments in agriculture would be welcomed. An idea that is still at the debating stage is leasing of land for agriculture by Kazakhstan and Tajikistan. It is probable that the two countries could be willing to cooperate on this issue.

Besides agriculture accessing Central Asian energy is crucial for India. The Turkmenistan-Afghanistan-Pakistan-India (TAPI) natural gas pipeline project backed by the Asian Development Bank (ADB) is important. It is hoped that the project would be completed as scheduled for 2016. Similarly, Indian involvement in the extractive industries is crucial. This can take shape in the form of upstream and downstream activities, construction of pipelines and their maintenance, upgrading and modernizing the existing refineries. What is of importance is to have a presence on energy scene. In 2009 the Oil and Natural Gas Corporation of India (ONGC) and its external wing the OVL and Mittal Enterprises on the one hand and KazMunai Gaz (KMG)a state run company of Kazakhstan signed an agreement for exploration in the Satpayev Block in the Caspian Sea. Construction of houses, hotels and roads ia another area where India can extend its cooperation. Another area is to transmit hydel power potential of Kyrgyzstan and Tajikistan to India via Afghanistan and Pakistan then to India. It would be worthwhile to explore the possibility of establishing an electricity grid here. Earlier India has successfully brought Uzbek electricity to Kabul via Phul-e Khumri. In fact the potential for cooperation in the economic field is vast. A major impediment to enhanced cooperation is the absence of direct connectivity. Although air links with these countries do exist and within three hours one can reach any of the capitals. There are nearly 7 to 8 flights from New Delhi and Amritsar to Ashgabat, Tashkent and Almaty. Direct flghts from New Delhi to Bishkek are likely to start soon. A cargo flight from Mumbai to Navoi an Exclusive Economic Zone (EEC) in Northwestern Uzbekistan is operational. It is hoped that a similar flight from New Delhi would commence shortly. Nevertheless, road or rail links are much more effective as bulk cargo can be transported. What are India's options?

Transport Linkages with Central Asia

From the Indian perspective the best option to reach out to Central Asia is to follow the ancient trade and transit route when Afghanistan was the hub of transport corridors. Afghanistan lay at the crossroads of major trade routes; east and west, north and south. In today's context the revival of this route involves India-Pakistan-Afghanistan-Uzbekistan-Tajikistan-Turkmenistan. However, this much preferred transport corridor is yet to emerge as a viable option. However, this option does not seem impossible as Afghan goods under the Trade and Transit Agreement between Afghanistan and Pakistan of 2010 are allowed to transit Pakistan up to Wagah border, but the reverse flow is not permitted.

In the prevailing situation the next best option is through Iran. It was during Iranian President Khatami's visit to India in January 2003 that India and Iran signed an agreement to allow Indian goods bound for Central Asia and Afghanistan a preferential treatment and tariff reductions at the Iranian port of Chah Bahar on the Makran coast. From Chahbahar a road link goes up to Zaranj on the Iran Afghan border. The Indian Border Road Organisation has constructed a 215 km road from Zaranj to Delaram on the Afghanistan's Garland Highway. From Delaram goods are transported to Mazar-i-Sharif via Herat and then to Naibabad on the border with Uzbekistan. Now that there is a rail link between Naibabad to Khairaton in Uzbekistan this route can be utilized. This option however, could do with better mutual understanding and efficient coordination among the three countries; India–Iran–Afghanistan. However, there are several options from Iran to Central Asia; a rail link from Mashhad (Iran) to Sarrakhs (Turkmenistan) already exists. The International North South Transport Corridor Corridor (INSTC) that connects Moscow and St Petersburg via Turkmenistan and Kazakhstan is operational, but could do with better coordination among the countries. For the INSTC to emerge as an efficient transport corridor, it is necessary that the rail connectivity between Iran and Turkmenistan and Turkmenistan and Kazakhstan is completed at the earliest. Iran is an important link. Iran has plans to build a rail link from Mashhad to Herat and later extend it to Kunduz in Afghanistan and then to Dushanbe in Tajikistan. Another concept is the Central Asia –Persian Gulf option that will give the CARs an opening on the Persian Gulf. In the prevailing situation it seems that the Iranian option offers India multiple choices to reach CARs as well as Afghanistan. What is essential is to generate the requisite political will. Another option often discussed is from Kazakhstan –Kyrgyzstan –China to Himachal Pradesh. Meanwhile Pakistan is also offering the CARs a transport corridor to Karachi or Gwadar, but its policy is to exclude India. Another possibility is to explore trilateral cooperation with the US in order to facilitate Indian access to Central Asia. Whichever transport option emerges for India to connect with CARs, either through Iran or Pakistan it would provide it as well as the CARs a multiple choice to reach out in the southern direction.

To conclude India faces an uphill task to connect with CARs. However, it is necessary not only to generate the requisite political will but also to demonstrate the loss of transit revenues to countries by pursuing an exclusive approach .

Session III

Second Paper

Mr Yuriy Makubayev

Economic Cooperation Between India And Kazakhstan: The Non Realised Partnership Potential

Since February 23, 1992 when diplomatic relations between India and The Republic of Kazakhstan were established, close cooperation in many fields is proceeding. Since January 24, 2009 our relations were raised to qualitatively higher level of strategic partnership. Taking into account the global processes occurring in the modern world, the special attention should be paid to bilateral cooperation and economic interaction. Economy is the key to development in international relations.

Kazakhstan is rich in mineral resources; it is the largest trading partner of India in the Central Asia. The most potential spheres of bilateral cooperation are power generation, manufacturing sector, metallurgy, agriculture, petrochemical industry and pharmaceuticals, IT-technologies, tourism, science, technical and military - technical cooperation, banking sector and other spheres of economy. Our country is interested in expansion of the Indian business presence in the economy of Kazakhstan. First of all, the priority is in the sphere of high technologies. The Kazakhstan Government is interested to diversify cooperation in energy sphere. The deepening of interaction with India carries huge potential in this area and mutually advantageous. Kazakhstan adheres to a multi-vector policy. Today its basic directions include cooperation with Russia, the USA, The European Union (EU) and the People's Republic of China (PRC). We welcome, promote and hope that India becomes the fifth vector in our policy. The leading position of India as the regional power and also its growing global influence, are of significance.

In Kazakhstan there are deposits of 99 elements of the Periodic table. It opens a huge field for cooperation in raw material sector. Taking into account, that bilateral trade between Kazakhstan and China is USD 25 billion with prospects for growth up to USD 40 billion by 2015. Against this background 600 million dollars trade level between India and Kazakhstan is inadequate and modest.

India is one of the largest importers of power resources and in view of its growing economy, internal demand for energy will only grow. India is one of the largest importers of oil. According to nongovernmental sources, up to 50 percent of Kazakhstan's oil-and-gas sector belongs to Chinese companies. In this respect, purchasing of 25 percent share in project "Satpayev" by ONGC Videsh Limited has got significant support in Kazakhstan. Moreover, ONGC Videsh Limited has also expressed desire to acquire share of ConocoPhilips (8.4 percent) in "Kashagan" the largest project.

A similar situation is observed in the sphere of nuclear power. Kazakhstan is the second richest state in the world on uranium explored reserves. But almost all export of this resource flows in China, providing growth of its nuclear power industry. India plans to increase fivefold energy production by Nuclear Power Plants (NPPs), which means that for the realization of this aim it needs nuclear fuel up to 8 thousand tons of uranium annually. According to expert forecast, demand of the country for nuclear fuel by 2020 will increase ten times. Thus, obligation of Kazakhstan to supply two thousand tons of uranium to India till 2014 within the framework of the Agreement on Cooperation in the sphere of peaceful use of nuclear energy which has great importance for both sides. But, it is obvious that the potential of cooperation in the field of nuclear power is not realized to the full. In fact, deliveries of a uranium concentrate from Kazakhstan to China are more than 25 thousand tons. Considering, that Kazakhstan plans to build nuclear power plant, the prospects of cooperation with India are tremendous.

Bilateral cooperation in financial sphere is also evident in Kazakhstan. For example, The Punjab National Bank has a control shareholding in Kazakhstan's "Danabank". The competition in the banking sector is a positive factor for economic development. Expansion of The Punjab National Bank's activity in Kazakhstan's financial market would be mutually advantageous. .

The joint space exploration is another potential direction for cooperation. In 2004 the Kazakh government initiated the program of space exploration; it is known that Indian space program is strong enough and able to give Kazakhstan necessary knowledge and technologies. Recently India became one of the most promising global leaders in the field of the space industry where three powers appreciably leading: the USA, Russia and China.

Cooperation in pharmaceuticals is of immense interest for Kazakhstan. India is the second largest manufacturer of medicines, and Kazakhstan imports medicines worth half a billion dollars. The joint venture is already functioning in the south of Kazakhstan.

IT-technologies are the most actual branch of cooperation. Indian companies such as 3i-Infotech, Tata Consultancy Services, NIIT, Larsen and Toubro, Punj LLoyd are represented in Kazakhstan. The Memorandum of Mutual understanding between the Indian and Kazakhstan groups of rapid response to infringement of computer security was signed for cooperation in the field of cyber-security. India is the world leading developer of computer programs; Kazakhstan needs technological know-how for creation of innovative economy.

Furthermore, it is necessary to pay attention to multilateral cooperation within the framework of such international platforms as the Shanghai Cooperation Organisation (SCO), the Conference on Interaction and Confidence Building Measures in Asia (CICA). Kazakhstan also appreciates the support of India in the accession of our Republic to the World Trade Organisation (WTO). Membership of Kazakhstan in the Customs Union opens attractive prospects for transit of Indian goods. The transit potential of our state which is located in the center of Eurasia, could open new markets for Indian business. Considering the aforesaid, the necessity for developing an efficient and an effective transport corridor project "North - South" needs no further explanation.

Thus, priority directions in our relations should be:

- **Mining industry.** Development of cooperation in this way is mutually advantageous, because Kazakhstan is capable of providing India the necessary resources of hydrocarbons raw, material and India is able to provide Kazakhstan assistance in the development of refining industry;

- **Power industry**. Our land is rich in the uranium which is essential for the functioning of Indian nuclear power plants. Moreover, India could assist us in realization of the project on construction of the nuclear power plant in West Kazakhstan; we also are interested in cooperation on production of nuclear fuel for NPP. Indian alternative power industry possess rich experience, green energy production from clean sources represents great interest for our country, it is especially actual in view of the tasks, which were put within the framework of carrying out EXPO-2017 in Astana;

- **Non commodity cooperation**. Especially in the field of high technologies with India can help Kazakhstan to diversify its economy. In particular, the most promising spheres for joint projects are computer technology, information technologies, an outer space exploration, biotechnologies, telecommunications, the chemical industry, construction;

- **Agricultural sector**. Considering, that deficiency of the foodstuffs accrues worldwide, it is expedient to create the joint agricultural enterprises of a full cycle, to develop and optimize means and methods with the purpose to increase efficiency;

- **Social sphere**. Kazakhstan pursues an active social policy. Our Government has emphasized the importance of education and public health services. Indian science is one of the leading areas; such as medicine and pharmaceutics which have obtained a global recognition. Hence, the Indian experience and knowledge possess great value for development of our country. It is necessary to create the Indian medicine centers in Kazakhstan, to develop joint scientific and educational programs (on a sample of the Indian Technical and Economic Cooperation (ITEC).

There are however, some obstacles in furthering bilateral trade and the intensification of economic relations.

- The main problem is logistics. Distance between our countries is relatively small, it can be overcome in three and a half hours by plane, which is comparable with Russia and China, but trade with India doesn't reach the proper level. We believe that the main obstacle in trade relations is a problem of transportation. Because of the inconvenient transport routes that runs through either China or through Iran's port Banderabas the logistic problems transforms the Indian export to Kazakhstan into uncompetitive goods. Thus, the cost of shipping a container from India to Kazakhstan through China is USD 6500; through Iran delivery cost is same and the delay in time is up to 2 months, it also reflects on quality of products, especially food. Transport problems have a reflection even in human exchanges between the two countries. For example, there is no direct flight service between Astana and New Delhi; you have to get one or two transfers. As a result flight takes 11 or 15 hours to reach the destination.

- Instability in Afghanistan and Pakistan also obstructs the traffic flow.

- Another obstacle for India is the economic competition with Russia and China.

- The existing base of bilateral agreements on branches of cooperation is insufficient.

- Finally, the excessive caution of Kazakh and Indian business community also prevents the development of economic cooperation. It is one of the reasons for the low level of mutual investment flows.

So, what have we have to undertake firstly is to intensify economic cooperation between our countries?

- Develop transport corridors within the framework of the 'North-South' project to solve the logistical problems. Or, if there was an agreement between Pakistan and India on the transit of Indian goods through the Pakistani Karakorum Highway and further to China and to Kazakhstan (this route has been successfully approved by Pakistan), the flow of Indian goods to Kazakhstan would be much larger and competitive.

- Expand a share of the Indian companies in the development of oil-and-gas deposits of Caspian Sea.

- Work together to solve the problems of oil transportation infrastructure.

- Intensify cooperation in the development of peaceful nuclear energy.

- Promote cooperation at the level of small and medium businesses.

- Involve Indian companies in Kazakhstan's financial market and vice versa.

- Increase the level of confidence-building measures for the Indian business in Kazakhstan.

- Development of the bilateral legal framework for industry collaboration.

Relations between India and Kazakhstan have a steady trend for further strengthening and expansion. India is an important participant in the implementation of significant initiatives of President Nursultan Nazarbayev, as the CICA and the Congress of World and Traditional Religions. But, economic relations should be a basis of bilateral cooperation. Kazakh-Indian Business Council has already been operating for nearly 19 years making efforts in this direction. It regularly hosts Kazakhstan-India business forums, exhibitions, fairs, etc. Mittal Steel Temirtau is an example of successful economic cooperation between our countries; the company has been operating in Kazakhstan since mid-1996.

In April, 2011 the Joint Plan of action on development of strategic partnership a 'Road Map' has been signed by Kazakhstan and India. We hope that its implementation will intensify cooperation between our countries.

Session III

Third Paper

Ambassador Parakhat H. Durdyev

Economic Engagement: Reconnecting Central Asia With India

It is a great pleasure to be here at this Institution and a privilege to address this forum and especially to share with you Turkmenistan's position on this very important subject on economic engagement with a special focus on reconnecting Turkmenistan with India. As I see it, this is a mutual aspiration, and it is natural that the two nations having had so much of bilateral interaction in the past going back to centuries, want to reestablish them in the areas of political, economic and cultural activities.

Before going into economic engagement issues between Turkmenistan and India let me just very quickly highlight some milestones in our relations.

Firstly, In terms of political cooperation, India recognized Turkmenistan as early as 20th April 1992, its Neutrality in 1995, and ever since has been supportive of our international efforts for example in 2008 when India co-sponsored a famous United Nations General Assembly (UNGA) resolution on reliable and stable transit of energy and its role in global sustainable development and cooperation. In its turn Turkmenistan supported India's non-permanent chair that ended in December 2012 as well as dozens other occasions in international organizations.

So far, we had a number of high level visits; the high point in recent times was the May 2010 State visit of Honourable President of Turkmenistan. In the course of the visit four Joint Intergovernmental Commissions (IGCs) on trade, economic, scientific and technological cooperation were signed of which the latest one being held in Delhi this January, India officially joined Turkmenistan-Afghanistan-Pakistan (TAPI) natural gas pipeline to become Turkmenistan-Afghanistan-Pakistan-India (TAPI). Unfortunately, the only prime minister of India to visit my country wayback was the late Narasimha Rao, in 1995 although we had regular inter-ministerial exchanges.

Secondly, from the very early times Turkmenistan is strategically located at the crossroads of civilizations, trade and transit routes and it became an important trade link between India, Central Asia, East and West via the Silk Route. At present we are connected by air though ground transportation presents many challenges as well as opportunities.

Thirdly, bonds between Turkmenistan and India date back to the times of Harappa and Indus Valley civilizations and the Bronze Age settlements in the South and West Turkmenistan at Merv, Nisa and Dehistan are well known. Well before and during Mogul India Turkmens played important roles in every aspect of life and Turkmen Gate is a testimony to that.

Currently, Indian film industry has a great presence in the country and the majority of Turkmen people cannot imagine their lives without Bollywood movies and songs.

So, over the past several years, our country together with its regional partners is actively working to promote the ambitious projects aimed at optimizing surface, sea and air transportation networks in Eurasia. Given the tremendous potential of the north-south, east-west transport corridors we believe that they have unlimited prospects in fostering economic and trade relations far beyond our region. Thus India may effectively become one of the major beneficiaries of these developments, as she pursues the goals of reaching out to its extended neighbourhood.

In this regard it is worth mentioning that there are a number of bilateral and multilateral arrangements like the agreement on the establishment of the multimodal international transport and transit corridor between Iran, Oman, Qatar, Turkmenistan and Uzbekistan, North-South Railway project connecting Iran, Turkmenistan,

Kazakhstan and Russia, as well as Sarahs-Meshhed railway link operational since 1995 and others.

Besides these international efforts Turkmenistan contributes to increase transit of goods to all available prospective markets through multimodal transport formats. Here I can only mention that these formats will include not only modes of transportations but more importantly Turkmenistan will have to engage its neighbourhood. We strongly share the common desire of all stakeholders that increased connectivity in this region will benefit both India and Turkmenistan and will also boost bilateral trade, which last year touched almost USD 190 million according to our Customs statistics. This is 277 percent more as compared to the previous year.

As mentioned above the energy and environmental security becomes as important as any other issues of global consequences. At this juncture we are witnessing tremendous and ever increasingly changing international environment. With all these challenges and opportunities in mind Turkmenistan looks forward to play, additionally, to that of a transportation hub, a major role in the area of international energy security as well. As one of the leading energy producers in the region it is obvious that we would like to have a system of international guarantees under the United Nations Organization, safeguarding not only our interests, but those of transit and end users of our energy resources as well. All these issues gained support in a more systematic and streamlined manner as the efforts of Turkmenistan have been within the above mentioned UNGA's Resolution.

Coming towards some of the specific aspects I can only briefly mention our progress in TAPI. Although we are lagging behind, nevertheless progress is there and in coming days you will witness some more positive developments especially pertaining to the establishment of the Special Purpose Vehicle or SPV– TAPI Ltd. The SPV, is meant to create an atmosphere of trust and provide all the participants equal rights as far as the future prospects of the Project is concerned. The company will be located in the UAE.

Mention must also be made that Turkmenistan's is a policy of diversification of energy export routes and in this context it is needless to say that the international system of secure energy transportation is a must of the day. Here we solely rely on the understanding of our partners.

In the vision of the Honourable President of Turkmenistan, he has emphasized the importance of raw materials like oil, gas and some other minerals, cotton and other agricultural produce but in broader term the diversification of the economy as a whole is essential. On top of that if we look at the intention of the Government to join the World Trade Organisation (WTO) in January 2013 – then it is obvious that security in our understanding is indeed a comprehensive concept that includes all aspects such as economic, environmental traditional security concerns etc.

As part of this comprehensive concept of security ecology has acquired its well-deserved attention. After the UN Conference on Sustainable Development (UNCSD), or Rio+20, Turkmenistan has been enforcing stricter ecological norms when it comes to the exploration of natural resources. Turkmenistan has enhanced its cooperation with the UN Specialised agencies on crucial issues such as the Caspian and Aral sea desertification, air pollution etc.

Communication industry in Turkmenistan is one of the most vibrant areas where the latest technologies are applied almost on a daily basis. The vision of the President of Turkmenistan is to send into the orbit its own communication satellite, which will provide a new level to national television broadcasting, the development of broadband access to the Internet and open the most modern and efficient way of communication. In this regard Turkmen-Indian Information Technology Centre established in Ashgabat in September 2011 must lead the way in training of personnel and India's quest on setting up a Central Asian e-network with its hub in India, to deliver, tele-education and tele-medicine connectivity, linking all the five Central Asian States.

Rapid growth of construction industry including construction materials in Turkmenistan can be a showcase to Indian construction companies capable of building world class structures at competitive rates, as construction activity is carried out especially housing construction within the National Programme on Enhancing Socioeconomic conditions in the villages. The Programme is applicable in towns, cities, districts and provinces for the period up to 2020. The potential for cooperation in this field is wide.

Today India is generously hosting more than a hundred Turkmen students on self-finance scheme, while ICCR provides some 5-10 slots per year and ITEC so far trained more than 300 people at a different short term courses. As compared to other countries these numbers are not to the extent that India could offer, the potential for such cooperation needs to be further explored and expanded. Nevertheless, we deeply appreciate this help and hope that in future additional slots will be allocated especially in much needed fields by our economy such as engineering and science streams.

At the recent IGC this January we agreed to hold the "Days of Indian Culture" in Turkmenistan in the second half of 2013 and the Indian side in its turn agreed to hold "Days of Turkmen Culture" in India in the first half of 2014. Besides these the Indian Embassy in Ashgabat is holding on a regular basis screening of Indian movies.

In conclusion, I would like to say that India's active presence in the region will contribute to stability and development in the entire Central and South Asia region. A cooperative approach for firmly involving Afghanistan into a more meaningful regional economic and security framework, would be beneficial for the entire region. One way is to work towards converting Afghanistan into a hub for trade and energy, connecting Central and South Asia and implementation of the TAPI pipeline is equally important. It will be of great benefit to Afghanistan, to Turkmenistan as well as to India and would contribute to our common prosperity.

Session III

Fourth Paper

Mr Evgeny Kablukov

Kyrgyz-Indian Economic Relations

Kyrgyzstan from the first day of its independence has tried to establish very good trade and economic relations with different countries of the world. Kyrgyzstan aims to create a favorable investment climate and is making efforts to provide beneficial conditions to foster further investment. A comprehensive programme of market reforms in Kyrgyzstan includes privatization, restructuring, price liberalization, full current market account convertibility, adoption of modern business legislation and great strides towards creating a dynamic financial sector.

Kyrgyz Republic has implemented a successful trade liberalization policy. It is the most liberalized trade regime among the Commonwealth of Independent States (CIS). It has been rewarded with the Membership of World Trade Centre (WTO,) which provides it with an open quota for inexpensive re-export. The two revolutions and especially political unrest of 2010 temporarily dampened the enthusiasm of international investors.

Nevertheless, many analysts now agree that Kyrgyzstan's economic conditions will continue to improve over the medium term. There were estimations of growth rates of four percent in 2011 and 5 percent in 2012. According to the data for the first two months of 2013 the growth rate was 8 percent. But we understand that a lot still needs to be done.

That is why Kyrgyz Government is keen to further develop trade and economic relations with countries of strategic interest as well as facilitate Kyrgyz export potential. Today, Kyrgyz export comprises nine groups of goods (fruits and vegetables, tobacco, cotton, textile, non-organic chemical goods, electric energy, cement, slate, electric bulbs) which constituted 52 percent of export in 2011. And together with gold total export operations was amounted to 96 percent of all exports.

What concerns India, according to Ministry of commerce of India, Kyrgyz-Indian trade totalled US$ 26.79 million in 2012. India's export to Kyrgyzstan was US$ 25.98 million whereas Kyrgyz exports to India amounted to only US$ 1.203 million. Apparel and clothing (both knitted and crocheted as well as knot-knitted and crocheted), leather goods, drugs and pharmaceuticals, fine chemicals, food oil, spices, vitamins, jewelry, household appliances and tea are some of the important items in the export basket from India to Kyrgyzstan. Kyrgyz export to India consists of raw hides, non-organic chemical products, medical equipment, and metal scrap, etc.).

The Kyrgyz-Indian trade is insignificant and constitutes only 0.1 percent of India's global trade. The major obstacles in Kyrgyz-Indian trade are stiff competition from countries in the neighborhood (in particular China, Turkey and the CIS and the difficulties flowing from the lengthy and unreliable surface trade routes, absence of direct air link between India and Kyrgyzstan, as well as difficulties in obtaining Kyrgyz visas etc.

In 1995 India had extended a USD 5 million line of credit to Kyrgyzstan; out of this USD 2.78 million were disbursed for four projects: a plant for manufacturing toothbrushes, a polythene bag manufacturing plant, a toothpaste production plant and a pharmaceutical plant. Kyrgyz side repaid USD 1.66 million and the balance amount was converted to grant.

Indian investments in Kyrgyzstan are marginal and are limited to plastic products and a pharmaceuticals manufacturing unit in the Special Economic Zone of Bishkek. In 2011 Jay & Jay Minerals of India acquired 20 hectares of land in the Special Economic Zone in Karabalta city for setting up a metallurgical plant with an investment of US$ 50 million. Electrosteel of India has evinced interest in setting up a ferro-silicon factory in Kyrgyzstan.

Tourism sector is of great interest for Indian tour operators.

Kyrgyzstan is comparatively new tourist destination for Indian tourists. Kyrgyzstan has a number of good hotels with all necessary facilities and comfort in Bishkek (Hyatt Regency – five star hotel, Ak-Keme, Golden Dragon, Silk Road Lodge and others) and in Issyk-Kul region (Aurora, Kyrgyzskoe Vzmorie, Raduga and others), where conferences, presentations etc. can be organized. To boost tourism Kyrgyzstan is going to renew direct flight Bishkek-Delhi-Bishkek from April of this year.

Many India assisted projects have been implemented in Kyrgyzstan during last 20 years. They are:-

Mini Dairy Plant. The Government of India gifted a Mini Dairy Plant to the Government of Kyrgyzstan in 1998 under the Indian Technical and Educational Cooperation (ITEC) Programme of the Ministry of External Affairs. The cost of project was US$ 500 000. The plant has a capacity to process 8 000 liters of milk. It can process dairy products such as pasterised milk, sour cream, butter and cottage cheese.

Plant for manufacture of toothbrushes. An amount of USD 486 00 was disbursed from the line of credit for supply of machinery for manufacture of toothbrushes by M/s Angelique International Limited, from New Delhi to a Kyrgyz company M/s Dostuk Joint Stock Company on a turnkey basis. The plant was commissioned in Jalalabad in southern region in 1998. The toothbrushes are being exported to Russia. The plant has won the award of the President of the Kyrgyz Republic for excellence quality and exports.

Plant for manufacture of polythene bags. This plant for manufacture of polythene bags (from low density and high density polyethylene) as well as polypropylene strings was set up by an Indian firm M/s Angelique International Ltd. for a Kyrgyz private firm M/s Ak-Tilek Joint Stock Company. An amount of USD 315 00o was disbursed from the line of credit setting up the plant on turnkey basis and was commissioned in January 1999 in Bishkek.

Indo-Kyrgyz Centre of Information Technology. The Government of the Kyrgyz Republic had requested India to set up an IT Centre in Bishkek. A MoU on the setting up of the IT Centre was signed in Bishkek on March 20, 2006. The IT Centre at the Kyrgyz

State University of Construction, Transportation and Architecture was inaugurated by H.E. Mr. Murli S. Deora, Indian Minister for Petroleum and Natural Gas, on 15 August 2007 during his visit to Bishkek to take part in SCO Summit.

Setting up of IT Centre at Osh State University. The Government of the Kyrgyz Republic requested for assistance from the Government of India to set up an Information Technology Centre at Osh State University. Feasibility study has been conducted and a final decision is yet to be taken.

Potato Processing Plant at Talas province. In August 2002 India announced the gifting of a food processing plant to the Kyrgyz Republic. The Kyrgyz authorities requested for setting up of a potato processing plant in Talas province. The total cost of the project is Rs. 108 044 000. The Plant was inaugurated by H.E. Mr. E. Ahamed, Minister for State of External Affairs, on 12 June 2012. The project is planned to produce 100 kg of conventional potato chips per hour and another 95.2 kg of dehydrated potato flakes.

Setting up of a Mountain Bio-medical Research Centre . The project was approved by the Government of India as a joint collaboration between DRDO and Kyrgyz National Centre for Cardiology and Therapy and allocated Rs. 6.5 crores for the project. The project was completed in June 2011 and the Centre was inaugurated by H.E. Mr AK Antony, Minister of Defence of India, on 5 July 2011.

Technical assistance under the ITEX Program, particularly in terms of human resources development, is the cornerstone of India's economic involvement in Kyrgyzstan. Kyrgyzstan has been allotted 80 slots on an annual basis for civilian training under ITEC. More than 800 professionals from Kyrgyzstan have received training in India since 1992.

Kyrgyzstan sees the following potential areas that should be implemented to give new impetus to expansion of Kyrgyz-Indian trade and investments:

• Establishment of an Indian Bank in Kyrgyzstan.

• Establishment of surface transport links between India and

Central Asia.

- Creation of an India Investment Fund.

- Setting up a trading house.

- Regular organization of Kyrgyz-Indian trade and investment promotional events.

- Liberalization of visa procedures.

- Renewing regular flights between Kyrgyzstan and India.

- Arrangements of preferential trading agreements.

- Availing of LOCs for high value projects.

Session – III : Discussion

Economic Engagement: Reconnecting Central Asia With India

Question - Is leasing of agriculture land by CARs to foreign countries/firms only an idea or has it been ever put to practice?

Response - Prof Nirmla Joshi, one of the panelists who had given this point during her presentation replied that leasing of land for agriculture to outside agencies is in discussion stage between Kazakhstan and some foreign NGOs. The issue had been stuck on the lease time – 49 or 99 years. Also, what kind of incentives will be provided to those who develop agriculture and how profit would be repatriated are some of the main contentious issues.

Ambassador Durdyev of Turkmenistan apprised that skilled labour from India is available in his country for varied jobs like construction and gas exploration. He said the issue of lease of land is worth exploring however, at this stage Turkmenistan was not thinking on those lines. Problems like repatriation of revenue etc can be overcome with a unified exchange rate. This point was endorsed by the representative from Kyrgyzstan as well. Ambassador Durdyev said that option of agricultural cooperation by leasing of land is not very strong as climatic conditions are different and that joint research was required before venturing into this sphere. He saw scope for cooperation in the area of water harvesting and its conservation.

Question - Are Defence factories of Soviet era in CARs still surviving? What is their range of production and if India could also contribute its expertise in their up gradation?

Response – The Kazakh participant Yuriy Makubayev in his reply said on weapon production there was a great potential for cooperating in the Defence sector and helicopter export from his country to India was one such field that could be furthered. He said that his country received nuclear weapons /material from the USSR. After the disintegration of the USSR the new regime in Kazakhstan sent back all nuclear bombs to Russia. His country only aims at developing nuclear energy for peaceful purposes.

Question - Is there any ban on export of Uranium from CARs?

Response – Yuriy Makubayev from Kazakhstan in his reply informed that his country had second largest deposits uranium in the world. He said that volumetric exports of Uranium to China are fifty times more than what they are for India. He said that China was interested to produce nuclear fuel as a joint venture with his country for her power stations.

Question - What can be the cooperation in the mining sector with India? What are the expectations of CARs with respect to heavy, medium and small industries?

Response – Yuriy Makubayev said in his reply that intellectual exchanges should keep growing between India and his country till the time communication routes are opened. He attributed logistics problems to poor trade between the two countries. He said his country was interested in diversification of their gas industry, mineral resources and computers. He said during interaction with his President; with experts etc. IT technology was at the focus of discussion.

Ambassador Durdyev of Turkmenistan replying on the issue said that there could be cooperation in the field. He mentioned that his country produces potassium fertilizer as a joint venture with some countries and India's fertilizer needs could be fulfilled by their exports. He said that his country would expect cooperation in steel production and weaver technology. Japan and Italy, he said, were leading in weaving industry and India could catch up with them. He emphasized that carpet weaving was in Turkmen genes and that India could gain from their experience. He anticipated India's cooperation in improving their high technology facilities including software facilities.

Evgeny Kablukov of Kyrgyzstan said that his country gives priority to small and middle scale industry rather than heavy industry. He expected that India should come forward and establish joint ventures in his country to be fully funded by India. Professor Joshi made a remark that mining of gold in Kyrgyzstan and designing of gold jewelry was a possibility as a joint venture which should be explored on priority.

Question - Is there any Shia- Sunni problem in the Central Asian societies and is religion controlled by the State within countries?

Response –Kablukov from Kyrgyzstan replied and said that all CARs were Sunni dominated and therefore there was no contradiction of two branches of Islam. He said that his country has State Commission on Religion which irons out any related differences and works towards social harmony. Giving out impact of Indian films on his country and the scope of cooperation in this field, Kablukov said that the scope was tremendous and that Indian film directors should make use of the natural beauty that his country offers by planning shooting schedules there. This would also help in promotion of Kyrgyz film industry also, he said.

Ambassador Durdyev stated that in 2005, his country adopted a law for religious groups and entities which gave ample space to people to practice their respective faiths. He said that majority of the Central Asian countries were Sunni and question of conflict did not arise. He said that religion had diluted during USSR era and people were now coming back to basics. He also sees a bright future for cooperation in tourism sector and stated that traditional/ ecological tourism was fast catching up in his country. He said that investments from India in this sector would be extremely important for both countries.

Yuriy Makubayev replying on religion said that majority of the people are Sunnis, but people from all nationalities stay in his country as government's policies are not discriminatory in nature. President Nazarbayev appoints people from minority communities in the government and there is no restriction on freedom of religion. The only restriction, he said was on radical use of the religion. He hoped that cooperation in tourism sector by India should be explored. The country is unique in a way and it has mountains, plains, deserts, sea and beautiful lakes. The country has historical sights and new and old cities for developing tourism. He said that his country would be interested in inviting medium and small business enterprises from India to boost its economy.

Question - China is eyeing Kyrgyzstan as its re-export hub, what could be the role for India in this?

Response – Kablukov responded by stating that that Kyrgyzstan was not a member country of Customs Union and therefore it is not possible that it could become Chinese hub.

In conclusion, the Chairman, Ambassador Phunchuk Stobdan, gave his concluding assessment on some of the issues, which he observed while being posted as Ambassador in Bishkek, Kyrgyzstan.

VALEDICTORY ADDRESS

Ambassador Phunchuk Stobdan (Retd)

Distinguished participants from Central Asia and India, Excellencies, Ladies and Gentlemen

It is an honour and privilege for me to deliver the valedictory address at this important seminar. I congratulate the United Services Institution of India (USI) for organizing the seminar, which gives us a good opportunity to share our thoughts and experiences, which I am sure, is beneficial for creating a friendly environment and understanding between India and people in Central Asian States. I understand that the deliberations have been to provide a holistic treatment to a range of issues covering India's engagement with the Central Asian States.

Let me first say that Central Asia is an old region with multiple layers of history imposed one over another; the last being the Soviet-era history, which has profoundly impacted the course of developments in the region.

It is noteworthy that the initial scenarios including the gloomy and negative once drawn for Central Asia fortunately have not come true. The transformations that have taken place during the last decades in each States have been somewhat smooth without much turmoil as each of them were able to protect their independence with varying degree of political and economic stability and success.

Central Asia, over the last two decades in general and recently in particular, is witnessing an unprecedented integration into the global economic and political mainstream, particularly on the world energy scene.

India's civilisational bonds with Central Asian countries as well as the Soviet legacy have been translated into warm and friendly relations. India's cultural heritage is deeply rooted in the Eurasian past. Indian traders and travelers had actively traded along the Silk Route and Buddhism had flourished across the vast Eurasian steppe. History is full of friendly interactions between India and Central Asia, through movement of people, goods and ideas, including spiritual interfaces that enriched us both. The fondness for Indian culture is expressed in Central Asia's deep interest in Indian cinema, music, and art. This interest intensified further in Soviet times.

India's relationship since 1990s have been marked by deepening relationships based on political, economic and technical cooperation as a partner, rather than a mere contender for the region's vast oil and gas resources. We have shared our experiences and expertise, built capacity and focused on training through our ITEC and other assistance programmes.

However, in the last few decades, India has been struggling to build economic links that match its political and cultural interaction. India's trade with the whole region is at a relatively low level of around 600 million US dollars. India faces some natural obstacles like limited land connectivity and the limited size of the Central Asian markets. India has thus not seen the sort of commercial interaction in Central Asia, which we saw in Southeast Asia, East Asia and West Asia. This has led to a joint quest for innovative answers, some of which we look upon this conference to throw up.

India is now looking intently at the region through the framework of its 'Connect Central Asia' policy, which is based on pro-active political, economic and people-to-people engagement with Central Asian countries, both individually and collectively.

The most important challenge for India is to get sufficient footing into Central Asian energy resources. Accessing the region's hydrocarbon and hydro-power resource would be of critical importance. Therefore, building a partnership with all the Central Asian countries is of primary interest.

I believe that India's active presence in the region will contribute to stability and development in the entire Central and South Asia region. In this analysis, we must factor in the regional situation and especially the challenge of rebuilding the Afghan nation. A cooperative approach for embedding Afghanistan into a more meaningful regional economic and security framework would have benefits for the entire region. One way is to work towards converting Afghanistan into a hub for trade and energy, connecting Central and South Asia. The landmark agreement for the construction of the TAPI (Turkmenistan-Afghanistan-Pakistan-India) pipeline has put the spotlight on the importance of Central Asia for India's future energy plans. It would also greatly benefit Afghanistan.

Central Asian countries could also gain from the techno-economic- potential of India, which could be accessed in cooperative, mutually beneficial partnerships. Your desire for diversifying hydro-power and energy export routes would correspond with India's quest for diversifying imports. India will be keen to invest in setting up downstream production facilities, instead of exporting raw materials out of the region through expensive pipelines. The approach could differ from those seeking exclusively to pump out Central Asia's riches.

It is also important to remember that India has never been prescriptive in its political approach. We represent our liberal democratic values, particularly in the Asian context. We believe in a nation building model based on participatory democracy, economic growth, building civil societies, pluralistic structures, ethno-religious harmony and the rule of law.

India thus stands ready for a deep, meaningful and sustained engagement with Central Asia. What is needed is that the Central Asian friends should create favourable visa conditions to accept India's benign presence. Perhaps the governments of all the five states will agree to simplify these procedures as early as possible.

India's 'Connect Central Asia' policy is consonant with its overall policy of deepening engagement in Eurasia, its policy of strengthening relations with China, with Pakistan, and building on our traditional relationship with Russia. India also engages with Russia and China under the RIC and BRICS framework. India hopes that its membership in numerous regional forums including at the SCO, would help India's renewed linkages with the region.

Collectively, India and Central Asian countries must also think about creating a cooperative security structure for maintaining peace in Asia. India's engagement in Central Asia, therefore, must be seen in the context of a quest for a world order which is multi-polar.

VOTE OF THANKS

Lieutenant General P K Singh, PVSM, AVSM (Retd)
Director, United Service Institution Of India

Thank you Ambassador Phunchuk Stobdan for delivering the Valedictory Address at this two day International Seminar on "Enhancing India and Central Asia Engagement: Prospects and Issues". I also take this opportunity to thank all our distinguished guests who have taken the trouble to be with us, to participate in this seminar and to enrich the proceeding covering the strategic, political and economic processes underway in our region. I am also grateful to each one of you to have participated wholeheartedly and given views so frankly. I am also grateful to your Excellencies the Ambassadors and diplomats for active participation and meaningful contribution. I must also take this opportunity to thank all members of the USI staff including the residency staff who have worked hard to make the event a success. I will be failing in my duty, if I do not thank the Ministry of External Affairs for having supported us whole heartedly.

www.ingramcontent.com/pod-product-compliance
Lightning Source LLC
Chambersburg PA
CBHW050534270326
41926CB00015B/3224